MARCO POLO

Tips

SAN FRANCISCO

CANADA

Washington   Montana   North Dakota

Oregon   Idaho   South Dakota

San Francisco   Wyoming   Iowa

Nevada   Nebraska

Utah   Colorado   USA   Kansas

California   Los Angeles   Oklahoma

PACIFIC OCEAN   Arizona   New Mexico

Texas

MEXICO

www.marcopolouk.com

← INSIDE FRONT COVER:
THE BEST HIGHLIGHTS

The best Insider Tips → p. 4

Best of … → p. 6

Sightseeing → p. 26

Food & drink → p. 60

SYMBOLS

INSIDER TIP	Insider Tip
★	Highlight
●●●●	Best of …
	Scenic view

Responsible travel: for ecological or fair trade aspects

(*) Telephone numbers that are not toll-free

PRICE CATEGORIES HOTELS

Expensive	over 200 dollars
Moderate	120–200 dollars
Budget	under 120 dollars

Prices for two people in a double room including breakfast

PRICE CATEGORIES RESTAURANTS

Expensive	over 36 dollars
Moderate	20–36 dollars
Budget	under 20 dollars

Prices are for a 2–3 course meal without drinks

On the cover: Cable cars – riding on the running boards p. 40 | Graffiti, art and coffee p. 17

CONTENTS

Shopping → p. 72

Entertainment → p. 80

Where to stay → p. 88

Street atlas → p. 118

MAPS IN THE GUIDEBOOK
(120 A1) Page numbers
and coordinates refer to the
street atlas and the map of
San Francisco and surrounding area → p. 132/133
(0) Site/address located off
the map
Coordinates are also given for
places that are not marked on
the street atlas
A public transportation route
map can be found inside the
back cover

INSIDE BACK COVER:
PULL-OUT MAP →

PULL-OUT MAP 🗺
(🗺 A–B 2–3) Refers to the
removable pull-out map

The best MARCO POLO Insider Tips

Our top 15 Insider Tips

INSIDER TIP **Stroll with a view**

Enjoy the wonderful views and history on the Golden Gate Promenade. Fly a kite, watch the kite-boarders perform their fantastic acrobatics or just join in and play soccer on the grass → p. 30

INSIDER TIP **Modern history**

The Contemporary Jewish Museum (photo right) never fails to fascinate visitors with changing exhibitions and events they can participate in such as a Refrigerator Magnet-Poetry-Slam-Workshop → p. 55

INSIDER TIP **Straight to you plate**

The Swan Oyster Depot serves delicacies from the ocean in an easy-going atmosphere → p. 67

INSIDER TIP **A mighty midget of a shop**

Two cheerful ladies prepare deliciously spicy – and amazingly inexpensive – sandwiches behind the counter of Saigon Sandwiches → p. 71

INSIDER TIP **Parla Italiano?**

The Caffe Trieste in the heart of North Beach (photo above) serves probably the best espresso in town and makes you feel like you are in Italy → p. 62

INSIDER TIP **Fine prospects for veggies**

San Francisco's best chefs make their purchases at the Ferry Plaza Farmer's Market and try out any unfamiliar delicacies at the countless stands → p. 78

INSIDER TIP **In the bag!**

Not only cycle messengers hang the trendy Timbuk2 bags over their shoulders when they struggle up and then shoot down the city's hills on their own or rented bicycles → p. 79

INSIDER TIP **The four elements**

Earth, air, fire and water set the tone in the Hotel Metropolis and there is also a library where you can relax → p. 96

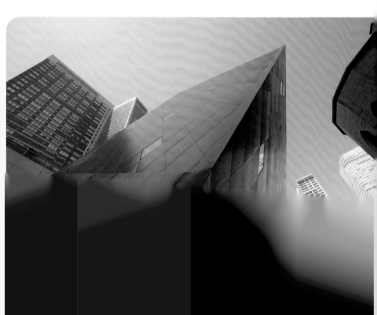

BEST OF ...

FOR FREE

● *Free concerts*
In spite of being so modern, San Franciscans still appreciate cultural attractions. The many free open-air concerts, classical operas and plays such as 'Shakespeare in the Park' are wildly popular → p. 86

● *Beach trip with a campfire*
This is free and fun, even if the water is not all that warm: at Baker Beach, children and dogs run for all they're worth, and young and old get together at wild Ocean Beach for picnics around enormous campfires → p. 28 and 43

● *Chinatown unplugged*
Chinatown's small streets (photo) are much more authentic than Grant Avenue that tourists like to visit. Stop off at the tiny Golden Gate Fortune Cookie Company and listen to the hairdresser next door playing his fiddle → p. 104

● *In Golden Gate Park*
Golden Gate Park is wilder than its pendant Central Park in New York but there is still a lot to do and discover here – and, it's all free! Show the Yanks how football is played back home or take part in a game of Frisbee golf → p. 48

● *Look inside the cable-car machinery*
Do you know how cable cars work? You can find the answer to this question by visiting the Cable Car Museum where you will see the cables, which are usually underground, spinning around enormous discs → p. 46

● *San Francisco tour for insiders*
What can you do after you've seen everything? Book one of the around 30 monthly tours organised by the San Francisco City Guides and have the locals show you places you never knew existed in the city → p. 114

●●●● Dots in guidebook refer to 'Best of ...' tips

ONLY IN SAN FRANCISCO
Unique experiences

● *The bridge over the Golden Gate*
The Golden Gate Bridge is probably San Francisco's most famous landmark. Of course, you can drive over it but you will be rewarded with the most magnificent views if you brave the winds and walk across (photo) → p. 29

● *Blocks of Victorian houses*
The *Painted Ladies* on Alamo Square are a must for all keen photographers. Go a little way up into the park and the downtown skyscrapers will tower up as the perfect background → p. 37

● *Ride the cable car running boards*
In this respect, San Francisco's cable cars are absolutely unique worldwide. Jump onto a running board, hold on tight and enjoy the rattling trip through all the districts of town → p. 44

● *Seals at Pier 39*
For many years now, hordes of seals have taken over a dock to the west of Pier 39. Today, the noisy troop has developed into a bigger attraction for many tourists than Pier 39 itself with all its shops → p. 50

● *Ice cream and cars on Lombard Street*
Is anything better than ice cream from Swensen's that first opened in 1948? With your ice cream firmly in your hand, you can watch the cars attempting to manoeuvre around the bends on Lombard Street → p. 49 and 63

● *Fried chicken feet anybody?*
Chinese cooks work painstakingly to prepare this and many other specialities that the waiters then wheel to the tables on trolleys for you to make your choice. A must; in New Asia, for example → p. 67

● *It's all fresh at Farmer's Market*
Not only the quality is first rate, the prices are too. Twice a week there is a fine selection of freshly harvested products at reasonable prices at Farmer's Market on Market Street – enjoy your meal! → p. 78

ONLY IN

BEST OF ...

● *Unadulterated shopping in Westfield Centre*

Get out your credit card and head off on a shopping spree to Westfield Centre. The restaurants will satisfy you at lunchtime and later a visit to a cinema will help you forget your aching feet and empty bank account → p. 77

● *To the ice rink!*

Sporting activities? This is also not a problem even if it is raining: there is an indoor ice-skating rink and bowling alley waiting for skaters and bowling fans next to the Zeum in the heart of the city → p. 48

● *Eat a crêpe and watch the world go by*

You can't stomach sport? Would you rather have an iced coffee and delicious crêpes? They are especially good in the Crêpe House – and *people watching* is thrown in free of charge → p. 62

● *Museum ships at Fisherman's Wharf*

Things were pretty hectic on Fisherman's Wharf during the Gold Rush era. Today the museum ships and submarine *USS Pamapanito* lying at anchor here tell of their past adventures → p. 49

● *Prison island with a view*

If you visit Alcatraz on a sunny day, you will find it hard to imagine just how inhumane conditions in this prison were. A visit when it is raining will give you a much better idea of the misery (photo) → p. 44

● *Modern art for all*

A visit to the San Francisco Museum of Modern Art (SFMOMA) with its permanent and temporary exhibitions of works by local and international artists is worthwhile even if you are not especially interested in such things → p. 58

RAIN

RELAX AND CHILL OUT
Take it easy and spoil yourself

● *Cosy calm in the Beach Chalet*
Those who find Ocean Beach too windy escape to the nearby Beach Chalet. There are a few deckchairs protected from the wind behind the restaurant – perfect for relaxing with a cocktail → p. 82

● *Massage with a punch*
You will be massaged by a team of well-trained specialists at True Massage & Wellness. If you are after a chic spa, this is not the place for you. But if you want a massage to pep up your body and spirit, this is just the thing → p. 84

● *Relax at a waterfall*
Get away from the hustle and bustle of the inner city – you will find the Yerba Buena Gardens a mere two blocks from Market Street. Greenery and a waterfall included (photo)! → p. 59

● *Acoustic relief*
Close your eyes and enjoy the music – visit a symphonic concert. Sometimes there are free rehearsals and performances at reduced rates in the early afternoon → p. 86

● *Oasis of beauty on Union Square*
The Earth & Sky Oasis is a day spa: a temple of relaxation where you can spend several hours. Acupuncture, massages, manicure, pedicure – all your beauty wishes will be fulfilled → p. 84

● *Land ahoy!*
A boat trip in the middle of San Francisco? Why not? It is possible to do this with a rowing boat or pedal boat on Stow Lake in Golden Gate Park – that you will find yourself sharing with a large number of ducks. The lake is not very big – you can just relax and drift for a while and, afterwards, have a lovely picnic on the grass → p. 41

INTRODUCTION

DICOVER
SAN FRANCISCO!

No matter how innovative, artistic, entrepreneurial and technically expert San Franciscans might be – anybody who tries to be super cool and calls their home town 'Frisco' should not be surprised if this is met with a look of contempt. In spite of all their progress, there is one thing the city dwellers have not thrown overboard: the pride in their city that has defiantly withstood dramatic events such as wars, earthquakes and politicians being murdered in City Hall since it became an independent community in 1850.

In addition, San Francisco – okay, you can call it 'San Fran' or 'The City' – is not just any old place but the fourth biggest city in California and, after New York, the city with the second-highest population density in the USA. And, it is also very beautiful:

Photo: Bay Bridge with the San Francisco skyline

with its hilly streets, Victorian houses and cable cars that seem to look down conde-
scendingly on their modern colleagues the hybrid-powered buses.

The city covers an area of 30,000 acres, extending over 50 hills that are frequently
so steep that cars are only allowed to park at tight angles to the slope. But, almost
every ascent is rewarded with a view of the Bay shimmering a dark blue in the soft
Californian light – except in summer, when the fog creeps into the city. You have a
fine view over San Francisco from the Coit Tower: to the south, you can see the
cluster of skyscrapers in the centre of town; to the west, the russet Golden Gate Bridge
glowing in the sunlight, while the dazzling steel Bay Bridge leading over the East Bay
to Berkeley and Oakland shines to the east.

San Francisco: an open-air theatre

San Francisco is nothing but an open-air
theatre with a great number of sights. But,
if you walk through the city, you will soon
realise that it has an absolutely unique
atmosphere. Keep your eyes wide open
when you are strolling around town, open all your senses and let the everyday life
and the great variety of characters in San Francisco work their charm on you.

There are now more and more digital displays at stops showing when the next bus
or train should arrive but they have not been able to do away with record delays. You

Haight-Ashbury – famous through the beatnik and hippie movement of the 1960s

often wait for half an hour and then three buses arrive at the same time. But that is part of the appeal of San Francisco: the city does not function perfectly but it has developed a special lifestyle of its own where everything flows – you only need plenty of time and patience.

The city still lives from the image of the creative-political beat generation around Jack Kerouac and Allen Ginsberg in the 1950s and the legendary 'Summer of Love' whose 45th an-

> **Freethinkers cultivate alternative lifestyles**

niversary will be celebrated in 2012. 1967 marked the birth of the hippie movement, with tens of thousands of flower children, dropouts and musicians, love, liberty and unity – drugs and sexual excess included. Today, many free-thinkers still live their alternative lifestyles in San Francisco. Many people from outside call the hippie district Haight-Ashbury, but here, people just refer to it as The Haight – even though the Haight-Asbury intersection has lost a lot of the magic it had in former times. It has been years since flower children could be seen sitting on the pavements.

Talking about pavements: even in tolerant San Francisco, some things are simply too much for the citizens and business people. Young 'bohemians' with savage dogs were causing so much trouble to the shop owners and people who lived on Haight Street that they decided to do something about it. The result: in spite of strong resistance

from most councillors, the majority of San Franciscans came out in favour of legislation in 2010 forbidding loitering between 7am and 11pm. Whether anything will change is another question.

There is an even more oddball story. In mid-2010, an increasing number of ticket inspectors were put on the busses to stop people travelling without paying. However, a number of illegal immigrants thought that these controls were being made by the US migration authorities and complained to City Hall that they had been terrified by this. The end of the drama – an official apology from the transport department for its behaviour!

Despite all the progress made since then, San Francisco has managed to preserve something of the lifestyle of the 1969 generation, namely the feeling that San Francisco is always tolerant and progressive. One in ten people living here states openly that he or she is homosexual. The mayor, Gavin Newsom, broke the law at the beginning of 2004 when he made it possible for 4000 gay and lesbian couples to marry – since then, the city, the state and its inhabitants have been quarrelling fiercely about legalising homosexual marriages. A district court in North California decided in favour of a suit made by supporters of homosexual marriages; however, the judgement was not executed due to objections raised by the court of appeal. The next referendum could take place in 2012 and it is possible that the US Constitutional Court will become involved.

There are approximately 1000 various ethnic groups in San Francisco and they all want to eat and live traditionally. It is often the case that individual districts have become the home of a certain group. In Chinatown, which stretches over Telegraph, Russian and Nob Hills, all of the signs are written in Chinese; only one block away to the north, you will find the best pizza in town in the Italian North Beach district; the Mission district in the northwest is dominated by Latinos and the rainbow flag of the gay movement flutters with pride over the Castro district.

Anything goes in San Francisco. Changes are accepted easily and difficulties quickly become challenges. This attitude has its origin in the Gold Rush days of the 19th century. The risk of earthquakes has also formed the collective psyche of being prepared to start anew. There were particularly strong rumblings in 1906 and 1989 and parts of the city had to be reconstructed. At the moment, the assumption is that there is about a 63 percent certainty that a *big one* will come before the year 2036.

The spirit of permanent change can also be recognised in the cityscape. In 1960 San Francisco was still mainly a harbour city and around 70 percent of the population were white, middle-class workers. Twenty years latter, the harbour complex had fallen into disrepair and the skyscrapers of the banks and enterprises in the service sector shot up. The cheap hotels for workers in the centre were flattened and the Moscone and Yerba Buena exhibition and culture complexes erected in their place. After heated discussions, most of the urban motorways that had been severely damaged in the 1989 earthquake were demolished. This was no loss. Today, the locals and tourists jog or stroll from Fisherman's Wharf to the Ferry Building and enjoy spectacular views of the city and Bay.

> **The spirit of permanent change can be seen throughout the city**

And the change continues. The San Francisco Stock Exchange is now home to a fitness studio, and an architect lives and works in the Mission Police Station – he helped transform what was once a very proper, white exterior into a colourful collection of political protest posters. In the mid 1990s, the South of Market (SoMa) area developed into the epicentre of the dotcom revolution. Not only the prices of Victorian houses that are so typical of San Francisco rocketed. Young entrepreneurs, graphic designers and programmers, lured by quick money, moved in where Mexican families, old hippies and pensioners used to live.

In spite of the internet bubble that burst in 2001, successful new start-ups such as Twitter and Dogster – a kind of Facebook for dogs – have come out of SoMa. In Silicon Valley companies such as Google, Yahoo, Facebook and YouTube tinker with Web 2.0, while Apple develops a never-ending flow of new iPads, iPods, iPhones and Macs.

The tourism sector suffered severe setbacks after the attacks in New York in September 2001 but now tourists are once again flocking to the city where TV programmes and cinema films are also being shot almost every week.

> **Successful start-ups emerge from South of Market**

Like the rest of the state and the USA as a whole, San Francisco is still fighting with the aftermath of the economic crisis. More than a dozen shops on three blocks of Geary Street, the best location in the inner city, are empty. Bus services are being cut back, social expenditure reduced and schools closed. Families are moving out of the,

All roads lead to the hustle and bustle of Fisherman's Wharf

still extremely expensive, city to the South and East Bay. The daily *San Francisco Chronicle* is struggling to survive, supermarkets are closing – in spite of annual profits running into the millions – to make room for owner-occupied flats. The city seems to be developing more and more into a kind of amusement park that the workers disappear from in the evening to make way for the tourists. But, despite everything, San Francisco is – and will remain – one of the world's most beautiful cities and its inhabitants will brave this and all future crises.

WHAT'S HOT

1 Accessories for the moment

The important thing is to attract attention People who wear these pieces definitely have something to talk about. For example, the way Stephanie Kim from *Dekkori* pimps absolutely normal court shoes into works of art for your feet by using ribbons, leather spats or metal *(www.dekori.com)*. The jewellery made by *Emiko Oye* (photo) is perfect for those who have remained children at heart; it is all made of Lego *(SF – Museum of Craft + Design, 201 3rd St.)*. And, Litter's chains decorate your ankles not your décolleté *(2152 Union St.)*.

Fixed-gear bikes 2

Minimalism on two wheels You can discover the streets of San Francisco without any chic extras. Fixed-gear bikes do without any gears and other accessories. *The Bike (650H Florida St.)* will tell you how you can put a fixie together by yourself. *Mission Bike* will create your bicycle exactly as you want it (766 Valencia St., photo). Another good address is *Box Dog Bikes (494 14th St.)*.

3 Pop-up eateries

Here today, somewhere else tomorrow The best chefs like to give guest appearances in other restaurants or open their own pop-up restaurants. This is the case with Alexander Marsh alias the 'Jet-set Chef'. You can find out when his restaurant is reopening under *www.thejetset chef.com*. Alexander Asegeb is also on tour with his African-Mediterranean cuisine *(www. radioafricachicken.com)*. Tommy Halvorson (photo) is currently making an appearance at a permanent address. He cooks at *The Corner (2199 Mission St., www.eatrestau rantblog.com)* every Friday.

Artists' circuit

Mission district 'The Mission' used to be called a mini Latin America. This past can still be seen in some places – at the market where yucca roots are sold and by the empanadas in baker shops' windows. Today this district is no longer only the new home of many immigrants from South and Central America but also of the artistic scene. The avant-garde sits around in coffee shops like the *Ritual Coffee Roaster* enjoying a cappuccino or latte and the latest paintings hang on the walls *(1026 Valencia St., www.ritualroasters.com)*. The Parisian *Kadist Art Foundation* has opened a branch just around the corner where it gives young artists space to let their imagination run riot. They also publish an art magazine here *(240 Folsom St., www.kadist-sf.org)*. All the graffiti around 24th street brings back memories of the Latino past *(www.missionmuralismo.com, photo)*. You can find out about what's happening in the district from *www.missionlocal.org*.

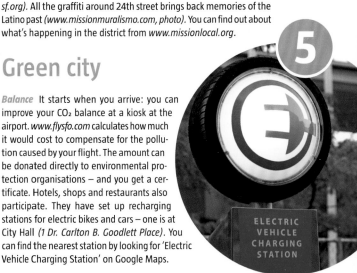

Green city

Balance It starts when you arrive: you can improve your CO_2 balance at a kiosk at the airport. *www.flysfo.com* calculates how much it would cost to compensate for the pollution caused by your flight. The amount can be donated directly to environmental protection organisations – and you get a certificate. Hotels, shops and restaurants also participate. They have set up recharging stations for electric bikes and cars – one is at City Hall *(1 Dr. Carlton B. Goodlett Place)*. You can find the nearest station by looking for 'Electric Vehicle Charging Station' on Google Maps.

ELECTRIC VEHICLE CHARGING STATION

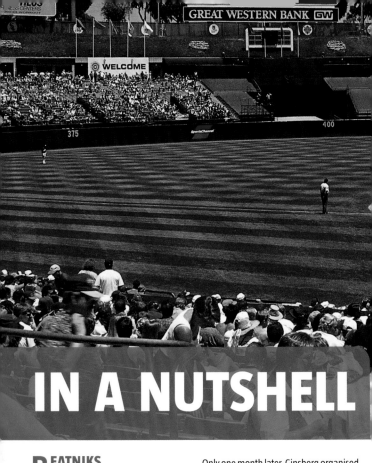

IN A NUTSHELL

BEATNIKS

'Yesterday, I met an interesting, bearded type in Berkeley who answered to the name of Snyder. He's into oriental Studies and is going to leave the Bay Area in a few months to become a Zen monk – just imagine, a real monk! He is laconic and stubborn, believes in Indian religions, but he is a warm-blooded animal with a funny beard, thin and blond, rides a bike in Berkeley and wears red corduroy trousers … an interesting person.'

This is how Allen Ginsberg described the author Gary Snyder in a letter to a friend written on 9 September, 1955. Ginsberg was visiting the Bay Area and stayed there.

Only one month later, Ginsberg organised a historical meeting of six selected poets in the Six Gallery. That is where he read his famous poem Howl for the first time – the 'San Francisco Beat Generation' was born.

A short time later, the West-Coast protagonists were joined by Jack Kerouac, William Burroughs and Gregory Corso, beatniks from the eastern seaboard. Beat works were intended to get to the heart of reality – without any varnish and almost grating. Thoughts were allowed to run free; the poets met in bars and cafés at North Beach to give more-or-less improvised readings of their works.

Photo: Baseball game

San Francisco is not a typical American city –
its steep streets, cable cars and inhabitants
from all walks of life show you that

CARE, NOT CASH

San Francisco has more homeless people than any other city in the USA. No matter whether they have chosen to be on the street or not, the city wants to help them find their place in society. Numerous organisations provide food, clothing and medical care. It is not a good idea to give money. Instead, have the left-overs from your dinner packed and donate this.

CULTURE PARTY

A different kind of *social networking* nowadays, cool San Franciscans go to museums in the evening – to sip a cocktail and attend dance performances and poetry readings. As many as 3000 guests make their way to the De Young Museum on Fridays, and things are similar on Thursdays in the California Academy of Sciences. Evening events are also held in

The wisps of fog make the Golden Gate Bridge seem to emerge out of nowhere

the Asian Art Museum, the San Francisco MOMA, the Exploratorium and the Fort Mason Center.

DOTCOM 2.0?

Today, the great dotcom crash of the years 2000 to 2002 when the NASDAQ non-financial stock market index plummeted from 5000 to around 1000 points seems to be almost prehistoric. The internet has once again become a billion-dollar business. San Francisco wooed the online news service Twitter with its approximately 350 employees to stay in the city by freeing it from taxes on salaries for six years. This meant that about 22 million dollars slipped through the city's fingers. In 2010, the online game developer Zynga (FarmVille, Mafia Wars) signed a seven-year lease for office space for its 2000 staff members that took up half of the Transamerica Pyramid. But these are two major exceptions – the majority of the 23,000 (!) start-up businesses in San Francisco and Silicon Valley such as Apple and Co. have outsourced their ideas to low-wage countries.

FOG

In one of his typical verbal broadsides, Mark Twain once said that 'the coldest winter I ever experienced was a summer in San Francisco'. Of all times of the year, the city is often covered by a layer of fog in the summer months. This is caused when the warm air over the land meets cold sea air to produce fog over San Francisco Bay. It is often cool and cloudy in the morning, but if the sun is strong enough, it sometimes forces its way through the fog by noon to make a brief guest appearance. But, at around 4 or 5pm, the fog takes over once again and it gets considerably cooler. It is a fascinating sight when the veils of fog sweep across the city like a flock of sheep in flight.

GREEN WAVE

San Francisco is a trailblazer in the areas of environmental protection and sustainability, waste separation and recycling. Plastic bags caught in the bushes and trees or swept into the Pacific through the sewers? Forbidden by law – many supermarkets reduce the bill if you bring your own bag with you.

And the public suburban transportation services rely increasingly on electro-buses and trams using energy from a hydroelectric power plant in Yosemite National Park. Since 2007, buses with internal combustion engines have only been fuelled with bio-diesel. Private persons can buy this from the *People's Fuel Cooperative* that produces this fuel using old vegetable oil they collect from local restaurants.

In San Francisco, those who find even that not environmentally friendly enough walk

BOOKS & FILMS

▶ **Tales of the City** – In the seven books of this series, the declared gay author Armistead Maupin describes the colourful life of a group of friends in the 1970s, '80s and '90s.

▶ **On the Road** – In his autobiographical novel (1957), Jack Kerouac is repeatedly drawn to San Francisco and gives a vivid depiction of the beat scene of those years.

▶ **Herb Caen** – The San Francisco Chronicle columnist wrote about *The City* from 1938 to his death in 1997 and invented the terms *beatnik* and *hippie*. His works are archived under *www.sfgate.com/columnists/caen/archive*.

▶ **Streets of San Francisco** – The classic crime series (1972–77) is the perfect way to get into the right mood.

▶ **The Rock** – This is just right for those who want to see a cable car explode (!):

Michael Ray made sure there was plenty of action on Alcatraz (1996).

▶ **Vertigo** – Alfred Hitchcock's 1958 thriller shows Fort Point, the Dolores Mission, the Palace of Fine Arts, the Pacific Union Club and other locations in San Francisco.

▶ **Dirty Harry** (1971), **Flight from Alcatraz** (1979) – Who is the real star: Clint Eastwood or San Francisco?

▶ **Milk** – Award-winning film drama from 2008 about the gay councillor Harvey Milk.

▶ **Bullitt** – Legendary: Steve McQueen's wild car chase during which Portero Hill turns into distant Russian Hill as if by magic (1968).

▶ **Mrs. Doubtfire** – The house Robin Williams' film family lived in is on the corner Steiner St./Broadway (1993).

or ride a bicycle. A traffic survey showed that the number of cyclists increased by 58 percent between 2006 and 2011. In 2009, 3.2 percent of all employees biked to work. Not a big number, but still five times higher than in the USA as a whole. Not to forget, all San Franciscans who use less gas for heating in winter are rewarded with a $25 one-way credit card.

SAN FRANCISCO ECCENTRICS

A crazy city like San Francisco obviously attracts a lot of crazy characters. For example, as early as in 1854, Joshua A. Norton proclaimed himself Emperor of the USA here. One of his heirs is Frank Chu who has been wandering around the inner city with his mystifying protest posters for some years now. Every day, they display new, nonsensical word combinations such as 'YETROJRENIUL' or 'KITROGRUNIOL PODCASTS'. In his own words, Chu is protesting against American presidents who 'swindled him out of 20 million dollars with the 12 galaxies'. Is Chu a performance artist who everybody likes or does he simply have a screw loose? It makes no difference, San Franciscans love him and keep him supplied with food and shoes so he can continue with his protests.

SOUTHERN-LIKE SUMMER

Not much sunshine in San Francisco? No problem, it's just a question of attitude. There is enough space for a few tables and chairs in the narrow inner-city streets such as Claude Lane, Maiden Lane and Belden Place – and the guests in the cafés and restaurants feel like they are in the south. Street life also flourishes near the Westfield Centre on Mint Plaza next to the former coinage factory – in addition to the restaurants, cafés and a nightclub, this is also the location of the weekly *Farmer's Market*.

SPORT STORIES

At *AT&T Park*, the *San Francisco Giants'* baseball stadium is so close to the Bay that, when a game is on, fans wait in their boats on the water and try to catch home-run balls hit out of the Park. Visitors who catch a ball in the Stadium are often greeted with a loud *Throw it back!* from the bad tempered *Giants'* fans.

Unbelievable but true: after a lousy start to the season, the eternally unlucky *Giants*

SPECTATOR SPORTS

Although the San Franciscans are active in their spare time, sometimes it is simply good to watch other people working up a sweat.

In *Candlestick Park*, the reasonably successful football stars of the *San Francisco 49ers (www.sf49ers.com | tickets from $25 at www.ticketmaster.com)* struggle for the football in a mixture of strategy and action.

The baseball players of the *San Francisco Giants (tickets from $25 | www.sfgiants.com)* are not much better but you don't really have to pay much attention to the game – a good meal, beer and a chat with friends are more important.

On windy days, you can watch the daredevil kitesurfers free of charge from *Golden Gate Promenade*.

actually won the *2010 World Series* – 56 years after the last time. Although only 29 American teams and one from Canada actually take part in the so-called 'World' Series, this in no way dampened the San Franciscans' joy. The city was on cloud nine for a few days and the celebrations reached their peak with a ticker-tape parade along Market Street and a reception for the team in front of City Hall that tens of thousands of fans flocked to.

The baseball legend Willie Mays also took part in the parade. He wrote history in the game between the *Giants* and the

but the end of his career was tarnished by his involvement in a doping scandal.

Things don't look as good for the *49ers*, San Francisco's football team. Many years have past since the team won a total of five *Superbowl* cups with stars like Joe Montana and O.J. Simpson. In the meantime, there is a proposal to move to Santa Clara 70 km (43½ mi) to the south where it is planned to build a new stadium by 2015. The present venue, Candlestick Park Stadium – where the Beatles gave their last concert in 1966 by the way – will probably be demolished then.

San Franciscans like going to family-run restaurants and shops such as here on Belden Place

Cleveland Indians in 1954 with an action that simply became known as 'The Catch': Mays fished the ball out of the air from an absolutely impossible angle, was almost pressed against the stadium wall but still managed to throw the ball back out of the catching movement as elegantly as a Greek javelin thrower. The Giants' pitcher Barry Bond was conspicuously missing from the celebrations. The former batter holds the league record of *762 home runs*

SUPPORT THE LOCALS

The San Franciscans are not especially fond of chains like McDonald's, Wal-Mart and Starbucks. They prefer to go to the small corner shops that are often run as family businesses – even if it does cost a few cents more. Here, the owners do not throw you out after a quarter of an hour to make room for new clients. And, the people you bump into in a *locally-owned place* are much more interesting.

THE PERFECT DAY
San Francisco in 24 hours

09:00am BREAKFAST AT A DINER COUNTER

It's easier to get moving after a good breakfast: The day in San Francisco's neighbourhoods begins with a hearty American breakfast in the *Pinecrest Diner (401 Geary St.)* one block away from Union Square. Sit at the counter and watch how speedily the cooks prepare the meals.

10:30am TAKE THE CABLE CAR

Walk one block to the east along Geary Street: get onto the *cable car* → p. 44 (photo left); if you buy a one-day pass you don't have to wait in the long queue at the terminus. It doesn't matter which line you take, both stop at the corner of Powell & Washington where you get off and walk two blocks east.

11:00am DETOUR TO CHINATOWN

Welcome to *Chinatown* → p. 43 or, more exactly, to Portsmouth Square the first public square in the city. This is a good place to start out on a tour through one of the oldest districts in San Francisco with its enchanting lanes, authentic Asian fruit and vegetable shops, and all the small and large shops selling goods of all kinds.

12:00pm AT FISHERMAN'S WHARF

Take the cable car from Powell & Washington towards *Fisherman's Wharf* → p. 43 (photo right); the Powell-Hyde line ends at Aquatic Park, the Powell-Mason line, three blocks to the south. Even if you don't feel liking visiting the shops at *Pier 39* → p. 50, you should at least take a look at the sea lions lolling about to the left of it. Is your stomach starting to rumble? No problem, just go to *In-N-Out Burger* → p. 70 and order your lunch; take it away and eat it on the steps of the Maritime Museum or directly on the beach. The view of Alcatraz and the Golden Gate Bridge will make it taste even better.

02:00pm THROUGH FORT MASON

Continue walking along the waterfront towards the Golden Gate Bridge until the road makes a right curve and leads up to a small rise. Follow the path through *Fort*

Get to know some of San Francisco's most fascinating aspects – right in the centre, at your own pace and all on a single day

Mason → p. 34 and take in the wonderful views of the city and Bay before catching the Muni Bus 28 towards Daly City Bart on Marina Boulevard.

02:30pm TO THE GOLDEN GATE BRIDGE

After a short trip through the Marina district, past Presidio with a view of the Letterman Digital Arts Center on the left, the bus reaches the *Golden Gate Bridge* → p. 29. Get off and explore the small park at the bus stop that is joined by a bridge to a section of the second-longest bridge in the USA.

04:00pm INTO THE FORMER HIPPIE DISTRICT

After all this nature, it's time to venture into the urban jungle. Take a taxi to the junction of *Haight & Ashbury* → p. 37 where the hippies used to get together in the 1960s. Today there are still many oddball characters ands shops here (photo). You can combat the first signs of weariness with a strong espresso in *The Grind coffee shop (783 Haight St.)*

06:00pm ALMOST LIKE MEXICO: MISSION DISTRICT

A change of scenery: walk or take Muni Bus 71 eastwards to Fillmore Street. Get on Muni Bus 22 there and off again at the 16th & Mission stop. *Hola!* Welcome to *Mission Street* → p. 42. Dive into the colourful buzz of activity a few blocks further south and experience Mexican hospitality in one of the many taquerías.

08:00pm NIGHTLIFT AT NORTH BEACH

After a short break to freshen up, it's time to throw yourself into the nightlife at *North Beach* → p. 43. How about a concert at *Bimbo's 365 Club* → p. 84, tasty baked goods at *Stella Pastry & Café (446 Columbus Ave.)* or just relaxed people-watching from one of the tables on the pavement in front of an Italian restaurant?

Take Muni lines 2, 3, 30, 38, 45, 91, or the Powell-Hyde or Powell-Mason cable cars, to the starting point Union Square stop

SIGHTSEEING

CITY WHERE TO START?
The area around **Union Square (124 C4)** (*⌂ P5*) with its many cafés, restaurants and shops is an ideal starting point and is easy to get to. The cable car will take you to Fisherman's Wharf in next to no time and you can reach the Ferry Building and Pier 39 with the historic L line. The Muni lines 2, 3, 30, 38, 45 and 91 also stop at Union Square. It's probably best to park your car in the underground car park there.

After New York City, San Francisco is the most densely populated metropolis in the USA. Around 815,000 people live in an area of approximately 125 km² (48¼ mi²) – but most of them have moved here from other states with about one third coming originally from other countries across the globe. This uniquely cosmopolitan flair can be felt everywhere – in restaurants, shops and in the streets.

Herb Caen, the long-time journalist of the *San Francisco Chronicle*, had good reason to call his city *Baghdad by the Bay*. With its more than 50 hills, San Francisco offers locals and tourists alike countless possibilities to make new discoveries. And a

Photo: View of the Bay from the city of San Francisco

Golden Gate, Alcatraz and noisy seals –
attractions from many cultures and lifestyles
make San Francisco vibrant and unique

study made in 2007 showed that, after
Los Angeles, San Francisco is where car
drivers waste most time in traffic jams.
Therefore, we can only advise you to walk,
take the bus or train, or rent a bicycle. If
you are passing through in a hired car, park
it somewhere and only use it if you want
to visit somewhat distant destinations
such as Marin Headlands or the lookout
point at Twin Peaks.

GOLDEN GATE BRIDGE/ PRESIDIO

**Presidio and Lincoln Park – these two
districts are part of the Golden Gate
National Recreation Area, a national park**

SAN FRANCISCO AT A GLANCE

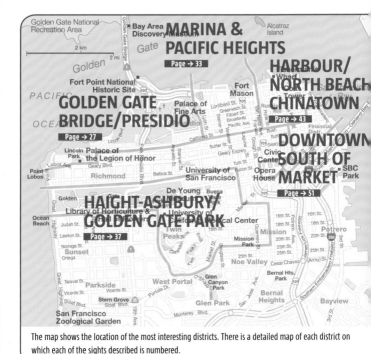

The map shows the location of the most interesting districts. There is a detailed map of each district on which each of the sights described is numbered.

that also includes the Golden Gate Park and Golden Gate Bridge, as well as Marin Headlands and Muir Woods to the north. In summer, the San Franciscans who live here and in the neighbouring residential areas often have to pay for the incredible view over the waters of the Bay with the dense fog that hangs over the city like an eiderdown on some afternoons and even hides the highest skyscrapers. However, if the weather is fine, they are compensated for this with a spectacular view of San Francisco and its Bay.

■ BAKER BEACH ● ∿
(121 D–E 2–3) (ⅅ E3–4)
Baker Beach is located between the Golden Gate Bridge and the villa district of Seacliff

where many famous people, including Hollywood star Robin Williams, live. The treacherous currents make swimming here not a good idea, but a picnic on the beach or a campfire in the evening can make you forget the hustle and bustle of the city. *Muni 29 – Sunset*

■ CLIFF HOUSE ★ ∿
(120 A5) (ⅅ A7)
Before Cliff House, built in 1863, became a day-trip destination for the whole city, it was the residence of US presidents and business tycoons. Cliff House, at the westernmost point of the city, burned to the ground twice before the many extensions gave it its present appearance. The House's restaurant *Sutro's (daily 11.30am–3.30pm,*

5–9.30pm) offers outstanding Californian cuisine and one of the city's most romantic sunsets. During the day, you can usually see pelicans, sea lions, dolphins and whales passing by. Live jazz on Friday evening; champagne buffet on Sunday *(10am–3.30pm)*.

You can have an American breakfast and burgers just a short distance away in the homely, reasonably-priced ☼ *Louis' Restaurant (daily 6.30am–4.30pm, Sat/ Sun to 6pm | 902 Point Lobos Ave., tel. 3 87 63 30 | Budget)* and also enjoy a wonderful view. *1090 Point Lobes Ave. | tel. 3 86 33 30 | www.cliffhouse.com | Muni 38 – Geary*

3 FORT POINT (121 E1) *(𝖒 F1)*

This army base, with its unique east-coast architectural style, was built between 1853 and 1861 and now houses an interesting museum where you can also see a film about the construction of the Golden Gate Bridge *(Fri–Sun 10am–5pm | free admission | www.nps.gov/fopo)*.

4 GOLDEN GATE BRIDGE ★ ● ☼
(121 E1) *(𝖒 E–F1)*

In the sunlight, it really has a golden glow; when it is foggy, it soars up out of the banks of mist; and it passed the hardest test – the 1989 earthquake – without any damage to speak of. It is, and will remain, a symbol of the city.

At the beginning of the 20th century, even the most daring engineers still thought that it would be impossible to build a bridge here. The Golden Gate – this was the name given to the channel connecting San Francisco Bay with the Pacific Ocean by Captain Fremont because it reminded him of the Golden Horn in Istanbul – had

MARCO POLO HIGHLIGHTS

completely different dimensions than the small inlet on the Bosporus. The water is up to 97 m (320 ft) deep and the force of the ebb and flow is a thousand times greater than that in the straits between the

Golden Gate Bridge: daring construction and landmark

Mediterranean and Black Sea. In spite of this, the city fathers commissioned studies for building a bridge in 1918. On 5 January, 1933, the chief-engineer, Joseph B. Strauss, witnessed the ground-breaking ceremony and construction was completed four years later on 27 May, 1937. An undisputed technical wonder, but there was a high price

to pay – 35 million dollars and the lives of eleven construction workers; 19 others survived after falling into safety nets.

The suspension bridge is 2.7 km (1.7 mi) long if one includes the motorway approaches on both sides. The main span measures 1966 m (4200 ft). It is supported by thick steel cables that would be 80,000 miles long if placed end to end – they could wind their way around the world three times! The two towers are around 227 m (745 ft) high and there is a distance of 67 m (220 ft) between the sea and carriageway.

There is a statue of Joseph B. Strauss who died one year after the completion of what was originally a highly controversial masterpiece at the southern approach to the bridge. *Toll $6, pedestrians and bicyclists free | Muni 28 – 19th Ave. to Toll Plaza or Golden Gate Transit busses from Market St., corner of 7th St North*, the INSIDER TIP Muni bus line 76 travels over the Bridge to Marin Headlands where it turns around and returns to the city; get off and enjoy the view!

5 INSIDER TIP **GOLDEN GATE PROMENADE** ☆
(121 E1–123 F1) (*M G–J2*)

The stretch of land between Aquatic Park and the Golden Gate Bridge is not as overrun with tourists as Pier 39 for example. This is where San Franciscans come all through the day to go jogging or take a stroll. The good 3 miles from Fort Mason to the Golden Gate Bridge are a really worthwhile excursion and offer spectacular views of the city and Bay. You reach the former post and military airport *Crissy Field (www.crissyfield.org)* by way of Aquatic Park, Fort Mason and the northern section of the Marina district that was erected on landfill. A few years ago, this was anything but beautiful; however, at the end of the last century, residents,

SIGHTSEEING IN THE GOLDEN GATE BRIDGE/PRESIDIO AREA

1 Baker Beach
2 Cliff House
3 Fort Point
4 Golden Gate Bridge
5 Golden Gate Promenade
6 Marin Headlands
7 Palace of the Legion of Honor
8 Presidio
9 San Francisco National Cemetery
10 Walt Disney Family Museum

schools and businesses planted more than 100,000 trees and bushes to restore the original appearance of the area.
This is where daring wind and kitesurfers set sail; the less adventurous are content to fly a kite in this often rather gusty area. A footpath on the western side leads to the Golden Gate Bridge *(see: Walking Tours, p. 98). Muni 28 – from Fort Mason, Golden Gate Transit 10*

6 MARIN HEADLANDS
(132 A–B 1–2) *(ⁿⁿ 0)*

It is well worth making a trip to this area if the weather is fine – even if you only visit the ☆ southern point of the enor-mous park complex with its wonderful view of San Francisco and the Golden Gate Bridge. If you have more time, you can explore the old fort, a lighthouse, a former rocket launching pad and the visitors' centre. Or take a hike along one of the numerous paths. *Daily sunrise to sunset | www.nps.gov/goga/marin-head lands.htm | Muni 76 – Marin Headlands*

7 PALACE OF THE LEGION OF HONOR (120 B4–5) *(ⁿⁿ B6)*

Does the Palace of the Legion of Honor seem familiar to you? That is quite pos-sible; it is a copy of the original in Paris, reduced by 25 percent. The very recom-

The Presidio Officers' Club, a visitors' centre today, brings back memories of Spanish colonial times

mendable museum is the home of a major collection of European and ancient art from the past 4000 years: paintings, pottery, sculptures and the more than 70,000 prints, drawings and books from the *Achenbach Foundation for Graphic Arts* – including works by Dürer, Gauguin and Kandinsky. There are also interesting temporary exhibitions. *Tue–Sun 9.30am– 5.15pm | entrance fee $10, also valid for the De Young Museum; free admission, first Tue in the month | www.legionofhonor.org | Muni 38 – Geary*

8 PRESIDIO ★ ☆ (121 E–F 1–4, 122 A–C 1–4) (*∅ E–J 3–5*)

This area with the breathtaking view in the northwest of the city was once the home of the Ohlone Indians and, after 1776, used as a military base by Spain, Mexico and then the USA. The army left the site in 1994 and it was placed under the ad-

ministration of the *National Park Service* and *Presidio Trust* three years later.

The former military buildings are now used as offices, schools and flats. In 2005, the director, George Lucas, moved into the *Letterman Digital Arts Center*, erected on the site of the erstwhile *Letterman Army Hospital*, with his film, special effects, and video games companies. Festivals, concerts and open-air theatre performances provide cultural highlights and exhibitions are held regularly in the visitors' centre, the former *Officers' Club* and probably the oldest building on the west coast of the USA *(daily 9am–5pm | 50 Moraga Ave.)*. *Muni 41 – Union, free PresidioGo shuttle service*

9 SAN FRANCISCO NATIONAL CEMETERY (122 B2–3) (*∅ G3*)

The graves of soldiers who have fallen in combat since 1854 are lined up in this soldiers' cemetery: 24.7 acres of uniform gravestones in the Presidio area. It is now a great honour to be buried here because this military cemetery is the only one in the city where funerals are still held. Normally, burials now take place outside the city boundaries – the city fathers having determined that land within the city is too expensive to be used as a final resting place. As early as in 1901 they ordered that all graves be removed form the former cemetery in Lincoln Park. The tombstones were used as building material. *Entrance McDowell Ave./corner of Lincoln Blvd. | Muni 41 – Union*

10 WALT DISNEY FAMILY MUSEUM
   (122 B2) (꘶ H3)
The ten spectacular galleries in a carefully adapted Presidio building that was formerly the army post's sports hall take you through the life of the creator of Mickey Mouse, Walt Disney. There are readings, performances and rare films from the Disney Archives. A must! *Wed–Mon 10am–6pm | entrance fee $20 | 104 Montgomery St. | Disney.go.com/disneyatoz/family museum | Muni 41 – Union*

MARINA & PACIFIC HEIGHTS

The Marina district is not even 100 years old and most of it is built on former landfill that is susceptible to soil liquefaction during strong earthquakes. The trendy types who live here ignore that and are compensated with being able to live so close to the water.
People who can afford to live in the million-dollar villas in the somewhat higher Pacific Heights district don't have to prove that they are wealthy. This is where you can find the homes of the writer Danielle Steele, the musician Lars Ulrich (Metallica) and Intel boss Paul Otellini. Have a INSIDER TIP look at the villas that are up for sale here. As everywhere else in San Francisco, they are usually open for potential buyers on Sundays. You can find more information about when and where they are open online or in the local newspapers.

LOW BUDGET

▶ Most of the museums do not charge admission on certain days – for example, entrance to the *Palace of the Legion of Honour* (120 B4–5) *(꘶ B6)* is free on the first Tuesday of the month. With the *Citypass ($69 | www.citypass.com)*, you can visit all the museums and attractions and also travel by bus, train and cable car for a week.

▶ If you find yourself in front of the *De Young Museum* (128 A1) *(꘶ G8)* but have no time for a visit, you should at least take the lift up to the top of the ↗ tower and enjoy the free panoramic view.

▶ Many people only use the map section of the tourist information material you find everywhere – but, there are also often coupons that make visiting museums and eating in restaurants less expensive.

▶ How do you feel about going to a gospel service? You will enjoy a visit to the *Glide Church Celebration* (122 C4) *(꘶ O6)* – infectious music and open to all. *Sun 9 and 11am | 330 Ellis St. | tel. 6 74 60 00*

■1 CHESTNUT STREET
(123 D2–124 C2) *(K–L3)*

There is a string of chic bistros and boutiques on Chestnut Street between Divisadero and Fillmore Streets – in the heart

Shops and a laid-back atmosphere:
Fillmore Street

of the Marina district where the residents don't only get dressed up on Saturday and Sunday when they go out to be seen in the pavement cafés. It is unusual in most large cities in the United States, but in San Francisco there are many such residential areas where it is possible for the people living there to walk to get all they need for their everyday life. *Muni 30 – Stockton*

■2 INSIDER TIP FILLMORE STREET
(123 E1–6) *(L4–5)*

Life is much more down to earth on Fillmore Street between Broadway and Geary Street than on Chestnut Street, for example. But the range of shops and restaurants is just as varied – and the residents are much more approachable making the chance of having a spontaneous chat much higher. *Muni 1 – California*

■3 FORT MASON
(124 A1–2) *(M2)*

Today, the former military base Fort Mason is a cultural centre where two dozen non-profit organisations, theatres, museums, a radio station, a library and many more institutions have their home. There are more than 15,000 different activities such as readings, exhibitions, performances, vocational training classes and festivals, which are attended by 1.6 million people, every year. A small example: in the *BATS Improv* theatre, actors improvise and develop their hilarious stories as the audience tells them *(Bayfront Theater | Building B, 3rd floor | tel. 4 74 67 76 | www.improv.org)*. The *SFMOMA Artists Gallery* represents more than 1300 North Californian artists and shows their works in eleven exhibitions each year *(Tue–Sat 11.30am–5.30pm | free admission | Building A North | tel. 4 41 47 77)*. The *Museo Italo-Americano* is the only museum in the USA devoted to Italian and Italo-American art and culture. In addition to exhibitions, festivals and lectures, it aims at making a contribution to

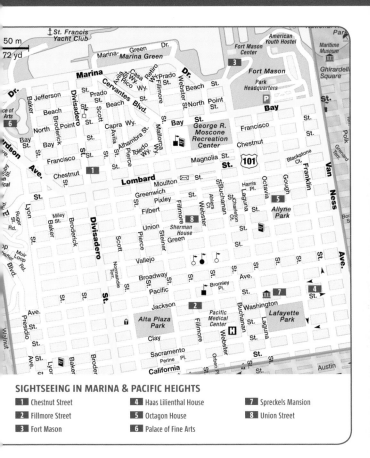

SIGHTSEEING IN MARINA & PACIFIC HEIGHTS

1 Chestnut Street
2 Fillmore Street
3 Fort Mason
4 Haas Lilienthal House
5 Octagon House
6 Palace of Fine Arts
7 Spreckels Mansion
8 Union Street

the preservation of the cultural heritage of Americans with Italian roots *(Tue–Sun noon–4pm | free admission | Building C | tel. 6 73 22 00 | www.museoitaloamericano. org).*

The Fort Mason Center is even an exciting, cultural adventure on cold, foggy days and you can fortify yourself by having lunch or dinner in the outstanding vegetarian restaurant ⚲ Greens *(Building A, see Food & Drink, p. 65). Marina Blvd. and Buchanan St. | www.fortmason.org | Muni 30 – Stockton, 10 – Townsend*

◢ HAAS LILIENTHAL HOUSE
(124 A3) (𝝮 N4)

This especially striking, completely furnished Victorian house is open to the public. It was built by William Haas, a grocery dealer from Bavaria in Germany in 1886, survived the 1906 earthquake undamaged, and is now the headquarters of the non-profit *Foundation for San Francisco's Architectural Heritage. Wed noon–3pm, Sat noon–3pm, Sun 11am–4pm | entrance fee $8 | 2007 Franklin St., near Washington St. | Muni 12 – Folsom/Pacific*

MARINA & PACIFIC HEIGHTS

5 OCTAGON HOUSE (124 A3) (*M3*)

This octagonal architectural gem from 1861 has also been painstakingly restored and fitted out with period furniture. In the middle of the 19th century, it was believed that eight-sided houses could contribute to a healthier, more content life. *2nd and 4th Thu and 2nd Sun of the month noon–3pm, except Jan | free admission | 2645 Gough St., near Union St. | Muni 41 – Union*

7 SPRECKELS MANSION (123 F3) (*M4*)

The sugar tycoon and philanthropist Adolph Spreckels built this white limestone beaux-arts palace with 55 rooms, including a French ballroom, for himself and his high-spirited wife Alma, 22-years his younger, in 1913. Today, this is the home of the bestseller author Danielle Steel. *2080 Washington St. | Muni 1 – California*

Palace of Fine Arts: grand building with an interactive Exploratorium

6 PALACE OF FINE ARTS (122 C2) (*J2–3*)

This is the only building erected for the *Panama Pacific Exposition* held to celebrate the completion of the Panama Canal in 1915 that is still standing today. The completely renovated rotunda and the neighbouring park and lake frequently provide the setting for weddings and film shootings. Also incorporating a theatre/concert hall and the *Exploratorium Museum (see: Travel with kids, p. 104)*. *Between Bay and Jefferson Streets | Muni 30 – Stockton*

8 UNION STREET (123 D3–124 C2) (*L–M 3–4*)

The Union Street shopping district between Steiner and Franklin Street is right in the middle between the Pacific Heights and Marina districts – you can tell this from all the antique dealers, jewellers, interior decorators, art galleries and beauty salons that have opened their doors here. This is where San Francisco's rich and beautiful go shopping as well as any number of visitors. *Muni 41 – Union*

HAIGHT-ASHBURY/ GOLDEN GATE PARK

Golden Gate Park, Haight-Ashbury, Alamo square and Mission District: less than 150 years ago the west of the city was still an area of high sand dunes that was quickly turned into residential areas and a large park when people stated flocking to San Francisco.

Locals and visitors recover from the hectic rush of everyday life; the museums, gardens, sunbathing lawns and sports complexes provide something for everybody.

The Haight-Ashbury district begins on the eastern edge of the park. In the 1960s, hosts of hippies, with guitars and drugs in their baggage, made their way here to lay the foundation for the 1967 *Summer of Love*. Even today, somewhat seedy char-acters offer their not-quite-legal wares for sale while new arrivals from all over the world look for unusual pieces of clothing, books and music in shops that are no less unusual. Alamo Square with its Victorian houses and the Mission District, the centre of Mexican and Latin American immigrants, are not far away.

1 **ALAMO SQUARE** ☀ (129 E1) (*Ш L7*)
If there was just one single view, this would be it – and it has been captured on thousands of postcards. Looking northeast towards Steiner Street from Hayes Street where the downtown skyscrapers form a backdrop to the charming row of Victorian houses called the ● *Painted Ladies*. Victorian is really not accurate. The only thing the architectural style has in common with the heyday of the English bourgeoisie, with their strict moral principles and romantic admiration for the British crown, is the period: the second half of the 19th century.

Queen Victoria was much less important for the style of what are also called the

MULTIMEDIA CITY TOURS

The *San Francisco Movie Tour* ($47 | www.sanfranciscomovietours.com) is not only something for film buffs. The three-hour tour takes you to the original locations of films such as *Vertigo, Mrs. Doubtfire, Bullitt, The Rock, Star Trek 4, The Maltese Falcon* and 70 excerpts from these films are shown on the bus – there is no better way to compare today's San Francisco with how it looked in years gone by.

Another unique way to get to know the city is on the *Magic Bus Tour* ($40 | www.magicbussf.com) produced by Jens-Peter Jungclaussen and the Antenna Theater, the creators of the Alcatraz Audiotour. This is anything but a boring history lesson. The 90-minute trip back to the 1960s is a wild mix of sightseeing tour, documentary film and theatre performance you can take part in. Screens are let down at historical sites to give an impression of how things were in the '60s – the race to the moon, beatniks and flower power were all part of it. A pretty flower girl also hands out 'LSD trips' – but without any active substances!

gingerbread houses than the carpenters who worked on them. Many had been to sea, had picked up ideas and models here and there on their journeys. And they also had no particularly strict moral codes: the spade-shaped cut-outs on a balustrade or roof gable were nothing other than a sign that gambling was carried out in the house. The ornamental bottles and hearts were also used for a kind of advertising: for bars and brothels.

The houses experienced a renaissance in 1970 and now the *Victorians* with their steep staircases and bay windows are the residences of the well-off and their owners guard them with their lives.

If you can't get enough of the *Painted Ladies*, you will find more Victorian houses on Lafayette Square, California Street and Liberty Street, as well as on Franklin Street and in the Presidio district. *Muni 21 – Hayes*

▣ CALIFORNIA ACADEMY OF SCIENCES ☺ (128 A2) (⌖ G8)

This building, designed by the Italian architect Renzo Piano, is the 'greenest' museum in the world today and relies on renewable energy to a large degree. It is the newest star in San Francisco's museum firmament.

Beneath its elegantly curved, grassed roof, the four floors of the building house an

SIGHTSEEING IN HAIGHT-ASHBURY/ GOLDEN GATE PARK

▣ Alamo Square
▣ California Academy of Sciences
▣ California Volunteers

Alamo Square – the beautifully kept Victorian *Painted Ladies*

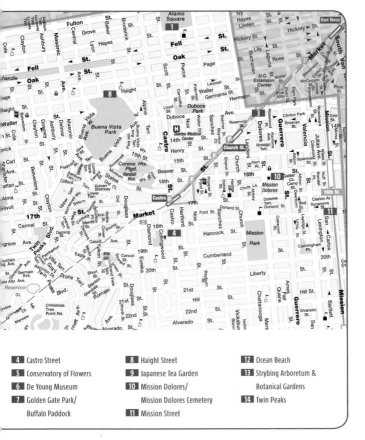

4 Castro Street
5 Conservatory of Flowers
6 De Young Museum
7 Golden Gate Park/ Buffalo Paddock

8 Haight Street
9 Japanese Tea Garden
10 Mission Dolores/ Mission Dolores Cemetery
11 Mission Street

12 Ocean Beach
13 Strybing Arboretum & Botanical Gardens
14 Twin Peaks

artificial rainforest, the *Steinhart Aquarium* with 38,000 sea creatures, a large coral reef, swamps and underwater tunnels, the spectacular *Morrison Planetarium* and the *Kimball Natural History Museum* with blue whale and Tyrannosaurus Rex skeletons, a Foucault's pendulum and interactive exhibits. Children can collect virtual insects using a Wii game console if they like. Fabulous! *Mon–Sat 9.30am–5pm, Sun 11am–5pm | entrance fee $29.95 | Golden Gate Park | www.calacademy.org | Muni 5 – Fulton*

3 **CALIFORNIA VOLUNTEERS**
(129 F2) (ﾉﾉ M8)

The sculptor Douglas Tilden immortalised the volunteers from California who took part in the Spanish-American war in 1898 with a winged horse, a goddess of war, a fallen and an unwounded soldier – the group of figures represents the divine force of the war after which the Spanish overseas possessions passed into the hands of the United State as a sign of anti-colonialism. *Dolores St./corner of Market St. | Muni F – Market*

4 CASTRO STREET
(129 E2–5) (*ⅅ L9–11*)

Somewhat more discrete than before but not completely gone – the gay bars, the showing off and the normal, everyday life of homosexuals, sometimes dressed in ties and suits, sometimes in leather and chains. If you want to get a closer impression of life in the gay community that has done so much to revitalise San Francisco and the city's politics, take the *Cruisin' the Castro Walking Tour (Mon/Thu 10am | $35 per person | tel. 2 55 18 21 | www.cruisin thecastro.com)*. Muni F – Market

5 CONSERVATORY OF FLOWERS
(128 B1) (*ⅅ H8*)

More than 1700 tropical plant species from all over the world compete for the light, air and water in the gigantic greenhouse of the Conservatory of Flowers that was opened in 1879 with orchids, carnivorous plants, palm trees and much, much more. The Victorian style palace of glass is the oldest hothouse open to the public in North America. *Tue–Sun 10am–4.30pm | entrance fee $7 | www.conservatoryof flowers.org | Muni 21 – Hayes*

6 DE YOUNG MUSEUM
(128 A1) (*ⅅ G8*)

The architecture of the monolithic, copper building in the heart of the Golden Gate Park is not undisputed – but it has a wonderful collection of treasures in its interior: more than 1000 paintings and 800 sculptures by American artists such as Grand Wood, George-Caleb Bingham and Richard Diebenkorn, as well as European painters including Claude Monet, Joan Miró and Andy Goldsworthy. In addition, there are collections of African, South American, Oceanic and textile art. *Tue–Sun 9.30am–5.15pm, Fri to 8.45pm | entrance fee $10, also valid for the Palace of the Legion of Honor | 50 Hagiwara Tea Garden Dr. | www.deyoungmuseum.org | Muni 21 – Hayes*

7 GOLDEN GATE PARK/ BUFFALO PADDOCK ★
(126 A2–128 C2) (*ⅅ A–H 8–9*)

The barely half-a-mile wide and 3-mile long green area is intended to be used for relaxation, sport and simply enjoying nature. Among the main attractions are the *California Academy of Sciences* and

TWO BELLS!

This is how cable cars work: a permanently moving cable runs underneath the middle track at a speed of exactly 9.5 miles per hour. The 7-ton carriages with seating for 34 passengers and standing room for another 34 on the California line, and 29 seats and space for 31 standees on the two Powell lines, run on the two outer tracks.

When the conductor rings the bell twice and calls out 'Two bells!' things start to move. The *gripman* (driver) pulls a heavy lever back and its lower end grips the cable like tweezers. When the cable travels downhill, the two have to brake like mad. In the extremely unlike case that all brakes fail, the gripman has an emergency brake: a wedge that he can ram into the middle track. If you want to get off, just say 'Next stop, please' to the *conductor* or *gripman*. Important: don't stand in the yellow zones – the *conductor* and *gripman* need the space for their really back-breaking manoeuvres.

Haight Street, corner of Masonic Avenue: a magnet for alternative lifestyles

the *De Young Museum (see description on p. 38 and p. 40)*. In addition, the park is a masterwork of the art of gardening. In reality, there should only be 'wind-driven' shifting sand dunes here. But after the city took over the area in 1868, the park director John McLaren, who remained in office for 56 years, planted bush after bush, and tree after tree until the sand had been conquered.

Today, buffalo graze in their own paddock at the west end of John F. Kennedy Drive. And, you can find pure relaxation on small ● *Stow Lake* in a rowing or pedal boat, or simply having a picnic on its shores in the company of all the families of ducks that live here. You will also discover a large number of tennis courts, bowling alleys, open-air chess boards and baseball fields; and the *Golf Course* with nine short, but very difficult, holes is open to the public. The 24 miles of paths can also be explored by bike *(Wheel Fun Rentals | 9am to sunset | 50 Stow Lake Dr. | tel. 6 68 66 99)*.

▣ HAIGHT STREET
(128 C2–127 F1) (🛒 J–M8)

The epicentre of the flower-power movement is divided into two sections. There are small restaurants, bars and record shops along Lower Haight between Divisadero and Webster Streets, while Upper Haight is the place to go for trendy boutiques and to see a few eccentrics as well. *Muni 7 – Haight, 71 – Haight-Noriega*

▣ JAPANESE TEA GARDEN
(127 F2) (🛒 F8)

The Japanese Tea Garden has been an established part of Golden Gate Park since 1894. This is a place where time seems to catch its breath: peaceful lakes, steep bridges, enchanted pagodas and mysterious Buddha statues transport visitors back to historical Japan. A visit when the cherry trees are in full bloom in mid-March is especially lovely. *Daily 9am–6pm | Mon, Wed, Fri free admission before 10am, at other times $7 | Muni 21 – Hayes*

10 MISSION DOLORES ⭐ /
MISSION DOLORES CEMETERY
(129 F2–3) (*M M8*)

The white Mission Dolores Church is one of 21 in California that were built one day's ride away from the next. It is also the oldest building in San Francisco and construction of it was completed in 1791. Indian paintings executed with vegetable colours of all this, the mission priests, the Mexican governor of Alta California, as well as the last Mexican Mayor of San Francisco all sleep peacefully *(daily 9am–4pm | $5 donation requested | 3321 16th St. | www.missiondolores.org). Muni F – Market, at the corner of Church & 14th Streets – change to Muni 26 at Fillmore or walk two blocks to the south*

Mission Dolores, built in 1791, is one of the oldest buildings in town

adorn the ceiling of the two-towered church and the altars and statues come from Mexico.

The dead who have found their final resting place here could even give less sensitive people cause to shiver. Thousands of speedily 'converted' Indians lie buried in unmarked graves. Dozens of men killed during the Gold Rush now rest beside several members of the oldest profession who possibly caused the quarrels that led to their miners' deaths. And in the middle

11 MISSION STREET
(125 E3–128 A6) (*M N8–11, O7–R4*)

Mission Street runs parallel to Market Street with its skyscrapers until it reaches South Van Ness Street. It curves to the right at 11th Street, passes under the Central Skyway – and enters a completely different world. This is where the Latin American *Mission District* begins. The signs in the restaurants and shops say *Se habla español* – Spanish spoken here. And the people there fulfil most of the clichés: they live in simple to shabby houses, listen to loud music and drive around in flashy cars. But be warned: even though the area seems to be cool – gangs can make it unsafe once you go past 16th Street. *Muni 14 – Mission*

12 OCEAN BEACH ●
(120 A6–126 A4) *(📖 A7–12)*

The windiest, wildest, foggiest beach in San Francisco is called Ocean Beach. In spite of the weather conditions, the city planners transformed the sand dunes into a residential area: the *Outer Richmond, Sunset* and *Parkside* districts came into being. Experienced surfers risk riding the waves here and people drowning here is not at all uncommon. Ocean Beach is at its warmest in September and October – maybe even warm enough for a short sunbathe but definitely for a stroll along the beach. *Great Highway | Muni N – Judah*

13 STRYBING ARBORETUM & BOTANICAL GARDENS
(127 F2) *(📖 F–G 8–9)*

The impressive botanical garden in the Strybing Arboretum is home to thousands of plants many of which can only be found here: local vegetation as well as flora from Asia, Africa, South America and Australia. *Daily 9am–6pm (April–Oct), 10am–5pm (Nov–March) | entrance fee $7 | www.sfbotanicalgarden.org | Muni 71 – Haight-Noriega*

14 TWIN PEAKS
(128–129 C–D4) *(📖 K11)*

On fog-free evenings, the view from Twin Peaks is quite simply phenomenal. The Spaniards called the two 902 ft (275 m) and 908 ft (277 m) high hills *Los Pechos de la Chica* – 'the maiden's breasts'. Twin Peaks Boulevard winds around the two. *Muni F – Market to Castro Station, from there Muni 37 – Corbett to the final stop, then a short, very steep, walk*

HARBOUR/ NORTH BEACH/ CHINATOWN

The area around Fisherman's Wharf, North Beach, Chinatown, Nob Hill and Russian Hill is full of contrasts. The Gold Rush period of 1848/49, when more than 600 ships and their crews were left behind in the harbour of San Francisco, is long past.

However, ★ *Fisherman's Wharf* is more than just a collection of T-shirt shops and restaurants. Museum ships lie at anchor at *Hyde Street Pier* while cruise ships tie up to the east of the touristic epicentre *Pier 39*. In spite of this, fisherman still go to sea from the north side of Jefferson Street and return with their nets full.

After years of silting, *North Beach* no longer lies directly on the water. Today, the streets are not dominated by Italian sailors but by Italian cafés and restaurant and cool bars. *Chinatown* is still home to one of the largest Chinese communities on the Pacific coast, but hardly any Russians live on *Russian Hill* – the Russian minority moved to the Richmond district many years ago.

Nob Hill was almost completely devastated in the 1906 earthquake but today is the site of many exclusive hotels and apartment buildings. The rich and powerful who used to live here rebuilt magnificent new villas in Pacific Heights to the west. *Polk Street* is a great place for you to get into contact with the relaxed San Franciscans in one of the many off-beat pubs and restaurants that serve food from all over the world.

■1 ALCATRAZ ISLAND ★ ●
(132 B2) (∅ O)

The Spanish named the rocky island *Isla de los Alcatraces* – Pelican Island – because it was the home of thousands of those birds. The Americans erected a fort there that they later turned into a military prison before it finally became the most feared jail in the United States. That was in 1934 when the public demanded a 'tiger cage' for the country's worst gangsters. The ice cold water, strong currents, machine gun towers and electronic detectors made sure that the prisoners were kept isolated. Al Capone sweat it out on this 'Devil's Island' as did 'Machine Gun' Kelly, 'Doc' Barker,

three men managed to escape in 1962, the government saw this as an opportunity to close the expensive penal institution. Today, Alcatraz is a part of the *Golden Gate National Recreation Area* under the administration of the *National Park Service*. You should count on your visit lasting around four hours. The crossing to the island starts from Pier 33. There is usually a great run on tickets, so be sure to book in advance. If you print your tickets from your computer, you will not have to queue up. *Daily from 9am, last crossing varies according to the season | ticket including audio-tour $26 | www.alcatraz cruises.com*

The most secure and most notorious prison on earth: Alcatraz

'Creepy' Karpis and the 'Birdman' of Alcatraz.

But there were quite simply not enough underworld bosses to fill the more than 300 cells and they started imprisoning simple car thieves and burglars on the island. The authorities found this ridiculous because of the costs – it would have been cheaper to rent hotel rooms. When

■2 CABLE CARS AND F LINE ★ ●

They are symbols of the city and mobile museums at the same time. There were often plans to mothball the cable cars but there was always an immediate uproar when this was announced. Legislation was passed in 1955: operation of the three lines can only be stopped with the approval of the majority of the voters – and

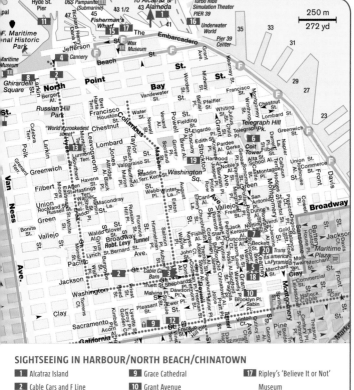

SIGHTSEEING IN HARBOUR/NORTH BEACH/CHINATOWN

1 Alcatraz Island
2 Cable Cars and F Line
3 Cable Car Museum
4 Cannery/Del Monte Square
5 Chinese Culture Center
6 Coit Tower
7 Columbus Tower
8 Ghirardelli Square

9 Grace Cathedral
10 Grant Avenue
11 Hyde Street Pier
12 James C. Flood Mansion
13 Lombard Street
14 Maritime Museum
15 Musée Mécanique
16 Pier 39

17 Ripley's 'Believe It or Not' Museum
18 Robert Louis Stevenson Memorial
19 St. Peter and Paul
20 Transamerica Pyramid

this is hardly likely to happen. You can INSIDERTIP avoid waiting for ever at the end of the queue if you walk a few stops and then get into the next carriage – or just jump onto the running board.

The Muni Transportation Service also uses historical vehicles on the F line – some from the 1920s. While some of the trams that make the journey from Fisherman's Wharf via Embarcadero and Market Street to the Castro district were made in San Francisco, many others actually come from other cities such as Newark, Philadelphia, Hamburg, Osaka, Melbourne, Moscow and Milan. They run 20 hours a day – not bad!

3 INSIDERTIP CABLE CAR MUSEUM ●
(124 C3) (*∅ O4*)

How does the underground cable work, what did the carriages look like before, how are they driven – this is where all these questions will be answered in great detail. *Daily 10am–6pm, Oct–March only until 5pm | free admission | 1201 Mason St. | Cable Car PH – Powell & Hyde, PM – Powell & Mason*

4 CANNERY/DEL MONTE SQUARE
(124 B1) (*∅ N2*)

The cannery, erected in 1907, was once the largest factory for tinning peaches in the world. Today there are many restaurants, shops and bars here. An eclectic mix of newcomers and old hands make music in the comparatively wind-protected inner courtyard while olive trees that are more than 130 years old provide shade for the visitors. *500 Beach St. | Muni F – Market*

5 CHINESE CULTURE CENTER
(124 C3) (*∅ P4*)

The centre aims at being a meeting place for the Chinese community and at fostering Chinese art and culture. The exhibitions change frequently but they all have a connection to Chinese culture. Visitors will also be interested in other activities such as the *Heritage* and *Culinary Walks* when expert guides take you on a stroll through the history and cuisine of Chinatown. *Tue–Sat 10am–4pm | free admission | 750 Kearny St., 3rd floor of the Hilton Hotel | Muni 15 – 3rd*

6 COIT TOWER ☼
(124 C2) (*∅ P3*)

137 m (460 ft) above sea level – that is only really impressive if the sea is right in front of you. This is the case here, and the 63 m (210 ft) high tower on 74 m (250 ft) high *Telegraph Hill* that soars up above the piers of San Francisco provides an

Hands-on technology among the operating equipment in the Cable Car Museum

INSIDER TIP especially spectacular panoramic view.

Lillie Hitchcock Coit, an eccentric millionairess, had a certain liking for firemen. When she was a child, she was the mascot of the team of fire engine No. 5. After her death, she left 100,000 dollars with the stipulation that the money be used to erect a tower in honour of fire fighters.

Some of the motifs of the pictures on the wall in the interior provide a complete contrast to Lillie Hitchcock Coit's wealth. In 1934, they were created in the purest form of proletarian realism by 30 painters who oriented themselves on the Mexican artist Diego Rivera. It is only a coincidence that the column-like shape of the tower resembles a fire hose. There is a lift to the viewing platform. *Daily 10am–7pm | entrance fee $4.50 | Telegraph Hill Blvd. | Muni 39 – Coit*

7 COLUMBUS TOWER
(124 C3) (*M P4*)

Some people are correct and call it *The Sentinel Building* and it is simply *Coppola's* for others – because this is the headquarters of the director and producer Francis Ford Coppola's businesses. *Café Zoetrope* on the ground floor serves Italian food and wine. You might even catch sight of some Hollywood celebrities here. The neighbouring *Transamerica Pyramid* creates a wonderfully photogenic contrast between the old and the new. *Columbus Ave./ corner of Kearny St. | Muni 20 – Columbus*

8 GHIRARDELLI SQUARE
(123 F1) (*M N2*)

Ghirardelli Square, located on the western edge of Fisherman's Wharf, is named after the chocolate factory owned by the Italian businessman Domingo Ghirardelli. His goodies are still sold – but no longer produced – here. Numerous restaurants and shops complete the picture. *Sun–Thu*

Illuminated view point high above the city: Coit Tower

10am–11pm, Fri/Sat 10am–midnight | 900 North Point St. | Muni 19 – Polk

9 GRACE CATHEDRAL
(124 B–C3–4) (*M O4*)

Could it be Notre-Dame? No, Grace Cathedral is a neo-Gothic copy with a beautiful rose window created in Chartres in France in 1970 that is illuminated from within at night. Grace Cathedral is the seat of the bishop of the *Episcopal Church*, one of the most important Protestant denominations in the United States. *Taylor St./corner of California St. | Cable Car C – California, Muni 1 – California*

⑩ GRANT AVENUE
(124 C2–4) (*ΩΩ P2–5*)

This was the first street in Yerba Buena and was named *Calle de la Fundación* – Foundation Street – at the time. It becomes narrower where it crosses Bush Street and passes through *China Gate* into the heart of Chinatown. You will be surprised when you see *Old St. Mary's Church* (1854) at the Grant Avenue junction; this used to be San Francisco's Catholic cathedral and is now the community church of the city's Chinese Catholics.

The atmosphere changes south of the Dragon Gate at the corner of Grant Avenue and Bush Street – this was a red-light district until the beginning of the 20th century but today there is a row of exclusive downtown shops next to each other. To the north, after the crossing with Columbus Avenue, you will find the cafés and bars of North Beach in what was once the Chinese slum district. To sum it up: if you walk down Grant Avenue from Union Square, it is elegant, picturesque, run down and, at the end, beautiful again, in turn. Today, the view from the formerly humble houses at the northern end of the street where it climbs up Telegraph Hill has made them extremely sought-after and almost unaffordable. *Muni 30 – Stockton*

⑪ HYDE STREET PIER
(124 B1) (*ΩΩ N1*)

The six ships lying at anchor at Hyde Street Pier – ranging from the Cape Horn sailing boat *Balclutha* to the ferry *Eureka* – create a scene from bygone days. National Park employees make boat parts by hand to replace those that have been ravaged by time in a workshop. *9.30am–5.30pm (June–Aug), 9.30–5pm (Sept–May) | entrance fee $5, ticket valid for seven days | Muni Cable Car PH – Powell & Hyde*

⑫ JAMES C. FLOOD MANSION
(124 C3) (*ΩΩ O4*)

A classic brownstone whose style would make it better suited to New York than

KEEP FIT!

Do you still have some energy to burn off? Then put on your trainers and jog up and down Potrero Hill – there are magnificent views of the inner city from ↘ De Haro Street **(131 D2–4)** (*ΩΩ Q9–11*) *(Muni 19 – Polk)*. If you prefer to have company for your sporting activities, you will find what you are looking for in the spacious ● *Golden Gate Park* **(126 A2–128 C2)** (*ΩΩ A–H 8–9*). Football and volleyball, frisbee golfers and boccia experts are always looking for new team players *(Muni 5 – Fulton)*. Or is water more to your liking? The beaches are open all year round and the *South End Rowing Club (www.southend.org)* organises a 1¼mi swim from Alcatraz to Aquatic Park **(124 B1)** (*ΩΩ N2*) every year *(Muni F – Market)*.

If the weather is bad, you can always visit the covered ● *Yerba Buena Ice Skating & Bowling Center* **(125 D5)** (*ΩΩ Q6*) for some sporting fun *(Muni 30 – Stockton)*.

San Francisco. The mansion from the year 1886 was the first brownstone house to be built west of the Mississippi by Augustus Laver for the 'Bonanza King' James C. Flood one of the men who had made huge profits in the silver boom and was able to pay 1.5 million dollars for his house at the time. It caught fire in 1906 but could be saved and was later renovated and extended. Today, it is the home of the *Pacific Union Club*, an exclusive association of well-heeled business men. Neighbouring INSIDER TIP *Huntington Park* is an invitation to catch one's breath and relax. *100 California St. | Cable Car C – California*

13 LOMBARD STREET ★ ● ☀
(124 B–C2) (*M N3*)

The crookedest street in the world – can only be driven down from the top. That is how steep it is and it also paved with bricks. It winds its way breathtakingly down the slope of *Russian Hill*. There are flower beds bordering every bend and the street makes a wonderful photo motif. If you decide to drive down Lombard Street, avoid the extremely busy weekends. The 'crooked' section starts at Hyde Street. *Cable Car PH – Powell & Hyde*

14 MARITIME MUSEUM
(124 A1) (*M N2*)

The art-deco building of the museum from the 1930s is modelled on an ocean steamer – the *Aquatic Park* forms the deck, complete with bow and stern. The visitors' centre and exhibits are currently located at the corner of Jefferson and Hyde Streets while restored underwater murals dazzle in the elegant white building *(daily 10am–4pm)*.

Not far away, ● ship enthusiasts will be interested in visiting the *USS Pampanito*; submarine fans can even spend a night on board *(daily 9am–6pm | entrance fee $10 | Pier 45)*. Right next door, the *SS Jeremiah*

Lombard Street – the crookedest street on earth

O'Brien, one of the more than 2300 Liberty Ships that served the merchant and war navy in World War II, lies at anchor *(daily 9am–4pm | entrance fee $10 | Pier 45)*.

A multitude of sea lions rub shoulders near Pier 39

15 INSIDER TIP ▶ MUSÉE MÉCANIQUE
(124 B1) (*∅ O2*)

What did our grandparents and great-grandparents do in their spare time around the turn of the past century? There were no shopping centres or TV, but playing with mechanical game machines and musical instruments was a popular way to pass the time. Edward Galland Zelinsky exhibits his enormous collection of these nostalgic devices – free of charge! *Mon–Fri 10am–7pm, Sat/Sun 10am–8pm | Pier 45, end of Taylor St. | www.musee mecanique.org | Muni F – Market*

16 PIER 39 ● (124 C1) (*∅ O–P1*)

Pier 39 is decorated colourfully with huge pots of flowers and has even more shops than Ghirardelli Square and the Cannery together. Since 1990, cheeky sea lions have taken over the landing stages to the west of the pier. In winter, there are between 300 and 900 of them here – then it becomes really crowded on the wooden platform and there are noisy squabbles over the best places day and night. At the weekend, the staff of the *Marine Mammal Center* provide information on the sea lions' lives. *www.pier39.com | Muni F – Market*

17 RIPLEY'S 'BELIEVE IT OR NOT' MUSEUM (124 B1) (*∅ O2*)

You will be able to gaze in astonishment at the world's smallest violin, strange gravestone inscriptions, chained fakirs and around 2000 other weird and wonderful objects collected by Robert LeRoy Ripley to form this museum. *Sun–Thu 10am–10pm, Fri/Sat 10am–midnight |*

entrance fee $16.99 | 175 Jefferson St. | Muni F – Market

DOWNTOWN/ SOUTH OF MARKET

18 ROBERT LOUIS STEVENSON MEMORIAL (124 C3) (*M P4*)

His book *Treasure Island* has thrilled millions. With *Dr. Jekyll and Mr. Hyde*, he explored split personalities. His personal adventure was completely different: impoverished and ill, he spent the years between 1878 and 1880 waiting for his adored Fanny Osbourne to be divorced. After that, the Englishman had only 14 years left to live before he died in 1894 on Samoa. A dream ship on a block of granite now forms a memorial to him. *Portsmouth Square/corner of Kearny St. and Washington St.* | Muni 41 – Union

19 ST. PETER AND PAUL (124 C2) (*M P3*)

This is where baseball star Joe DiMaggio married his first wife Dorothy Arnold and where he posed for photos on the steps leading up to the entrance after his wedding to his second wife Marilyn Monroe. The church, which originally catered for Italian immigrants, is run by the Salesian order of Don Bosco, the largest Catholic religious order after the Jesuits. *666 Filbert St.* | Muni 41 – Union

20 TRANSAMERICA PYRAMID (125 D3) (*M Q4*)

At the beginning, it was extremely controversial, but in the meantime this building has become one of the city's landmarks. And the figures of the building designed by William Pereira and completed in 1972 are truly impressive. The last of the 48 storeys covers only one eleventh of the area of the ground floor. It is more than 850 feet high – no other conventional building, only the television tower – is higher. *600 Montgomery St./corner of Columbus Ave.* | Muni 41 – Union

Civic Center, Financial District and South of Market – this is the way we see big American cities in films and on television: canyons of skyscrapers, hectic people, car horns and police sirens.

You will find all of this in the inner city, San Francisco's downtown, but it seems somewhat more relaxed and not quite as dogged as in New York for example.

Even in the city's financial district, benches and the bases of monuments invite visitors to take a rest and admire the old and new skyscrapers. The workers and people out for a stroll in town fortify themselves for the rest of the day in coffee shops and small restaurants. South of Market Street, the *Westfield Shopping Center* that was opened in 2006, the *Moscone Center* exhibition hall, the *Metreon* shopping and cinema centre, the *Yerba Buena Center for the Arts* and the *Museum of Modern Art* attract many visitors – it is impossible to be bored here.

1 101 CALIFORNIA (125 D3) (*M Q4*)

Its architect is one of the most famous in America – and he always designs something out of the ordinary. Philip Johnson created this building that is also known as the *Hines Tower* in the early 1980s as something like a prelude to the post-modern. The base of the skyscraper creates the impression of a symbiosis between a hothouse and a triangle of stone. A cylindrical tower, whose exterior is covered with prisms that refract the light thousandfold, rises up from this understructure. In combination with the base, two steeply rising – also triangular – flowered terraces

Abraham Lincoln, the great opponent of slavery, sits in front of City Hall

what questioning gaze with which he looks down at the people passing by make this different from most of the other Lincoln statues, where the slaves' liberator usually appears to be rather grim. When Haig Patigian created the memorial in 1926, the worries of many people were not unlike those of the slaves: economic depression, want and poverty. *City Hall at Civic Center | Muni 5 – Fulton, 2i – Hayes*

3 ASIAN ART MUSEUM
(124 B5) (⌘ O6)

The old building in Golden Gate Park was torn down as a result of earthquake damage and the Asian Art Museum has now resided in the time-honoured former City Library opposite the City Hall since 2003. It was worth waiting for. Approximately 15,000 exhibits are displayed in an area covering about 43,000 square feet. The Musée d'Orsay is just one of the many other buildings designed by its architect, the Italian star Gae Aulenti. The result: the integrity of the beaux-arts building was preserved and, at the same time, freshend up with sophisticated glass elements. *Tue–Sun 10am–5pm, Thu 10am–9pm | entrance fee $12 | 200 Larkin St. | www. asianart.org | Muni 21 – Hayes*

4 AUTODESK GALLERY ⏱
(125 E3) (⌘ R4)

This gallery, which was built to strict energy-saving measures, is a mixture of chic design museum and an understated permanent commercial programme. It illustrates the path from the design to the final product: Autodesk's design software has been used for cars, guitars, a cathedral, the Bay Bridge and even the Academy of Sciences. *Mon–Fri 9am–5pm, tours every day at 12.30pm | free admission | 1 Market Street – Suite 200 | usa.autodesk.com/ gallery | Muni F – Market*

form an unconventional courtyard where water splashes in a fountain made of white granite. *101 California St. | Cable Car C – California*

2 ABRAHAM LINCOLN MONUMENT
(124 B5) (⌘ N 6–7)

There he sits, the 16th President of the United States of America who was shot in 1865 and therefore did not live to see the end of slavery, even though he experienced the reconquest of the southern states. Seated in front of the main entrance to the City Hall, the friendly, some-

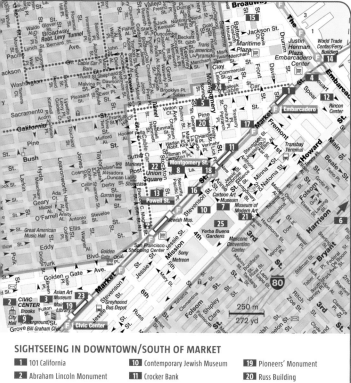

SIGHTSEEING IN DOWNTOWN/SOUTH OF MARKET

1. 101 California
2. Abraham Lincoln Monument
3. Asian Art Museum
4. Autodesk Gallery
5. Bank of America
6. Bay Bridge/Treasure Island
7. Cartoon Art Museum
8. Circle Gallery
9. City Hall/Civic Center
10. Contemporary Jewish Museum
11. Crocker Bank
12. D'Audiffred Building
13. Dewey Monument
14. Ferry Building
15. Fountain of the Four Seasons
16. Market Street
17. Mechanics Monument
18. Pacific Telephone Building
19. Pioneers' Monument
20. Russ Building
21. San Francisco Museum of Modern Art (SFMOMA)
22. Union Square
23. Vallaincourt Fountain
24. Wells Fargo History Museum
25. Yerba Buena Gardens/ Center for the Arts

5 BANK OF AMERICA
(125 D3) (*ሙ* P4)

This is where its heart beats and when the 228 m (748 ft) high, jagged skyscraper with its 52 storeys was constructed in 1972, it was the most powerful bank in the world. The colour of the granite on the façade changes with the incidence of light from blood-red to almost black. But, there is no question about the sculpture on the plaza created by the Japanese artist Masayuke Nagare. It is pitch black and, soon after the building was completed in 1962, it became commonly known as *The Banker's Heart. California St. between Kearny and Montgomery St. | Cable Car C – California*

6 BAY BRIDGE/TREASURE ISLAND ☼
(132 C2) (*Ø S4–5*)

The *San Francisco-Oakland Bay Bridge* is the sister of the *Golden Gate Bridge*. It became world-famous as a result of the 1989 earthquake when 15m of the construction broke and the upper carriageway collapsed onto the lower one killing several drivers. The earthquake-resistant reconstruction of the eastern section has been in progress since 2002. A single-tower bridge is expected to be completed in 2013 – with several years delay and at a cost of 6.1 billion instead of the originally budgeted 780 million dollars. The connection to Oakland, which was constructed between 1933 and 1936, is more important for traffic than its more famous pendant. Approximately 100 million cars cross the 13.6 km (8.5 mi) long construction that is closed to pedestrians. Magnificent views from the former Treasure Island military base. *$4 toll towards the city*

7 CARTOON ART MUSEUM
(125 D4) (*Ø Q5*)

The San Francisco area has always acted as a magnet for cartoon talents. The only cartoon museum in the United States not only exhibits caricatures but also explains historical and social changes with the help of cartoons. *Tue–Sun 11am–5pm | entrance fee $7 | 655 Mission St. | www.caroonart.org | Muni 30 – Stockton*

8 CIRCLE GALLERY (124 C4) (*Ø P5*)

Do you know the Guggenheim Museum in New York? This is the building that preceded it. This gallery designed by Frank Lloyd Wright was the first, small execution of a building with a ramp winding upwards inside it. It is on Maiden Lane – which, in spite of its harmless name, was a street of prostitution 100 years ago. *140 Maiden Lane, near Union Square | cable car PH – Powell & Hyde*

9 CITY HALL/CIVIC CENTER
(124 B5) (*Ø N6–7*)

The then mayor, Willie Brown, took advantage of the situation after the 1989 earthquake not only to have the City Hall – that was first opened in 1915 – seismically protected but also to return its roof to its original condition, including goldsmith work to the sum of half a million dollars. The building with its more than 93 m (305 ft) high dome – higher than that of the Capitol in Washington – was designed by Arthur Brown Jr., the architect of the Opera House and Coit Tower.

An impressive marble staircase rises up in the middle, and the hall where Joe DiMaggio and Marilyn Monroe were married in 1954 is on the third floor. With a bit of luck, you can also see the mayor's antechamber and reception room on the INSIDER TIP highly recommended tour of the building *(Mon–Fri 8am–8pm, tours Mon–Fri 10am, noon, 2pm | 1 Dr. Carlton B. Goodlett Place).*

Main thoroughfare with a view – Bay Bridge links San Francisco with Oakland

The Civic Center with a library, opera house, theatre and museum was completely rebuilt after the earthquake of 1906. The City Hall was designed in the Renaissance style and the surrounding buildings followed a similar pattern although construction lasted from 1915 (City Hall) to 1936 *(Federal Office Building)*. Only the *Davies Hall* – the home of the *San Francisco Symphony Orchestra* – that was opened in 1980, was built in a modern, earthquake-resistant style to provide a conscious contrast. *Muni F – Market, 21 – Hayes*

10 INSIDER TIP CONTEMPORARY JEWISH MUSEUM (125 D4) (*Q P6*)

The Museum, founded in 1984, has the goal of throwing light on Jewish culture, history, art and philosophy through permanently changing exhibitions and special events. The exhibits, discussion groups and lectures proved to be so popular that a new building of 75,000 ft² became necessary and its doors were opened in June 2008. It is not a coincidence if the building reminds you of the Jewish Museum in Berlin or the Felix Nussbaum House in Osnabrück: all three were designed by Daniel Libeskind. The American star architect flanged a new building with the dramatic lines that are so typical of his work onto a transformer station of Pacific Gas & Electric that Willis Polk had designed one year after the great earthquake of 1906. The activities of the Contemporary Jewish Museum appeal to all age groups – families can try their hand at make puppets with members of the National Theater of Israel, and teenagers can explore the museum's architecture while their parents visit the current exhibition. *Thu 1–8pm, Fri–Tue 11am–5pm | entrance fee $10 | 736 Mission St. | www.thecjm.org | Muni 30 – Stockton*

11 CROCKER BANK (125 D4) (*Q Q5*)

Old and new: the headquarters of the financial institution rises up on the corner of Montgomery and Post Streets just as it did in the founding years. But it was integrated into a tower in the mid-1980s and therefore appears like an inclusion in a piece of amber. The tower, a slender needle coated with pink marble, rises up 212 m (696 ft). A four-storey shopping arcade with an arched glass roof has been erected between the two sections of the building – a fascinating combination. The roof garden is an oasis of green in the heart of the busy city. *Post St./corner of Montgomery St. | Muni F – Market*

🖽 D'AUDIFFRED BUILDING
(125 E3) (*∅ R4*)

This especially lovely Victorian building, that differs from most of the others through the homogeneity of its style, was named after its builder Hippolyte D'Audiffred. It is partly used for offices and shops and it is therefore possible to visit some sections of it inside. *Mission St. at Embarcadero | Muni F – Market*

🖾 DEWEY MONUMENT
(124 C4) (*∅ P5*)

This is another monument glorifying the Spanish-American war of 1898. On the block of granite, a winged, crowned goddess of victory with a trident in her hand storms towards Admiral Dewey who conquered the Spanish fleet in the Battle of Manila Bay and drove the Old World out of the Third World to benefit the New World. *Union Square | Cable car PH – Powell & Hyde, PM – Powell & Mason*

🖿 INSIDER TIP FERRY BUILDING
(125 E3) (*∅ R4*)

The Ferry Building at the end of Market Street (1896–1903) was a major junction from where boats set out across the Bay before the two large bridges – the Bay Bridge and Golden Gate Bridge – were built. Before 1936, as many as 50 million passengers got off the ferries from the north and east here every year – many of them came from the station of the trans-continental railway in Oakland. In 2003, the Ferry Building and its 70 m (230 ft) high bell tower were completely renovated and now invite visitors to take a relaxed stroll through its cafés, a bookshop, restaurants and shops selling locally-produced food. *Embarcadero/corner of Market St. | Muni F – Market*

🖽 FOUNTAIN OF THE FOUR SEASONS
(125 D3) (*∅ Q3–4*)

The four seasons are symbolised by four bronze columns of different sizes that represent spring, summer, autumn and winter. The water flows from the columns

Ferry Building will make shoppers' and gourmets' hearts beat faster

into a small, tranquil pond. François Stahly created the fountain in 1967. It is the centre piece of the – often overlooked – park on Sydney G. Walton Square that, with its other art works, manicured lawns, high pine trees and a circle of poplars, is the perfect place to take a rest. *Corner of Jackson and Front St. | Muni F – Townsend*

16 MARKET STREET
(125 E3–127 D5) (*L9–R4*)

Market Street is diagonal and intrudes on the usually right-angled layout of the city. It is 30 m (100 ft) wide and cut through many pieces of land when it was laid out; that is why the land surveyor who planned it, Jasper O'Farrell, was almost lynched in 1847.

It has long been one of most important traffic axes in San Francisco. The Muni underground trains and the Bart line that unite the city with the residential areas on the other side of the Bay run beneath it. These means of transportation also provided the infrastructure that was necessary to build the skyscrapers in the Financial District on both sides of the north-eastern section of Market Street in the 1970s. Less attractive: the area between 6th Street and Van Ness Avenue with its many homeless people and junkies. The south-western end is not completely built up. The terrain where the mountain crest winds its way up between Corona Height and Twin Peaks is often too steep for houses to be built. *Muni F – Market*

17 MECHANICS MONUMENT
(125 D4) (*Q5*)

Just a minute; are we still here in the classic land of capitalism? Five oversized labourers working with a sheet of iron. Donald Tilden created this monument of proletarian realism in 1900/01 in memory of Peter Donahue. The Irish immigrant and

smith built the first printing press, the first tramline and founded the San Francisco Gas Company. *Battery St./corner of Market Street | Muni F – Market*

Market Street: shops, skyscrapers and the historical F line

18 PACIFIC TELEPHONE BUILDING
(125 D4) (*Q5*)

This is one of the most beautiful skyscrapers and it was built in 1925. At the front, the long lines strive upwards; from the back, San Francisco's first skyscraper is constructed asymmetrically. There are plans afoot to use the building as a luxury hotel and private flats. *140 New Mont-*

gomery St., near Market St. | Muni F –
Market

19 PIONEER'S MONUMENT
(124 B5) (*000 O6*)

The city's largest monument is dedicated
to the pioneers, those adventurous and
courageous people who conquered the
American continent. A goddess with a
shield and spear pays homage to four
groups of white newcomers who were
victorious over the perils of the sea, the
overland route and the Indians. A certain
James Lick donated the gigantic monument. His name has its place alongside
those of the settlers and soldiers who sub-
jected the New World to their will. *Hyde
St./corner of Fulton St. | Muni F – Market*

typical of many buildings of the period.
*235 Montgomery St., near Pine St. | Muni
Cable Car C – California*

21 SAN FRANCISCO MUSEUM OF
MODERN ART (SFMOMA) ★ ●
(125 D4) (*000 Q5*)

The main attraction of the Museum of
Modern Art lies in its collections of ab-
stract Expressionist art and photography.
The problem was always the same: the
rooms were quite simply too small and
works from the collection could only be
shown on a rota basis. This could mean
that works by Francesco Clemente and 125
of his contemporaries were on display, and
then 188 photos from Liselotte Model's
pre-war American and European œuvre,

The SFMOMA: the artworks on display are every bit as spectacular as the architecture

20 RUSS BUILDING
(125 D4) (*000 Q5*)

This early 31-storey skyscraper built in
1928 was the highest building in San
Francisco for a long time. In spite of its
symmetry, it displays the decorative elements, mainly in the neo-Gothic style, so

followed by Chicago art from between
1965 and 1985.
This situation has now become much better. The museum was able to move into
a $60 million new building designed by
the Swiss architect Mario Botta that, with
its architectural form and sophisticated

lighting, has now become a genuine cathedral of modern art.

The San Francisco MOMA's collections include works by famous west-coast artists including Mark Rothko and Jackson Pollock, a considerable number of paintings by the French master Henri Matisse, some paintings by Joan Mirò and Pablo Picasso, as well as an interesting selection of works by the German artists Max Ernst, George Grosz, Ernst Ludwig Kirchner and Kurt Schwitters. And, the architecture and design departments have set new standards for the rest of the world. *Fri–Tue 10am– 5.45pm, Thu 10am–8.45pm | entrance fee $18, Thu 6–9pm, half price, first Tue in the month, free admission | 151 3rd St. | www. sfmoma.org | Muni 30 – Stockton*

22 UNION SQUARE
(124 C4) (*🛵 P5*)

The city's heart beats in the centre of an elegant shopping district and is, at the same time, a small botanical garden with palm trees and exotic flowers. This is the place to met friends, watch people passing by, or for just dosing in the sun. The monument is a memorial to Admiral Dewey's victory over the Spanish fleet. The square was given its name because here, shortly before the outbreak of the Civil War, demonstrations were held in favour of the northern states, the so-called Union. *Muni 45 – Union-Stockton, Cable Car PH – Powell & Hyde and PM – Powell & Mason*

23 VALLAINCOURT FOUNTAIN
(125 D3) (*🛵 Q–R4*)

This is how things were in the 1970s – at least, in the field of architecture: down-to-earth, practical, functional. Armand Vallaincourt created a monument to those years with his *Québec libre!* by stacking more than 100 concrete blocks on top of one another. *Justin Herman Plaza | Muni F – Market*

24 WELLS FARGO HISTORY MUSEUM
(125 D3) (*🛵 Q4*)

The Wild West was really an exciting place to be – a pioneering history full of gunfights and stagecoach chases. You can experience all of this once again on two floors of the headquarters of the oldest bank in California and largest transport company in the West, Wells Fargo Bank, founded in 1852. Badges and guns, *gold nuggets* from the Gold Rush period and prospectors' tools, as well as the large *Wells Fargo Overland Stagecoach* from 1865, a post coach with room for as many as 20 passengers. *Mon–Fri 9am–5pm | free admission | 420 Montgomery St. | Cable Car C –California*

25 YERBA BUENA GARDENS ●/ YERBA BUENA CENTER FOR THE ARTS
(125 D5) (*🛵 K–L 8–9*)

Only a few years ago, most people did not dare go to Yerba Buena Gardens even though it is only two blocks away from Market Street. The green space between the Metreon, San Francisco Museum of Modern Art and the Zeum was shared by drug dealers and the homeless. In the meantime, the sunny park has been cleaned up considerably and is now one of the San Franciscans' favourite spots.

In spite of all its beauty, it is quite possible that you can walk right past the *Yerba Buena Center of the Arts*. But that would be a real mistake! There is a steady stream of exhibitions by the most popular artists in town in the exhibition halls to the east of the Park. The – mostly experimental – works not only aim at appealing to the eye but also at fascinating all of the senses and, at the same time, being thought provoking *(Thu–Sat noon–8pm, Sun noon– 6pm | entrance fee $7, first Tue in the month, free admission | 701 Mission St. | www.ybca.org). Muni 30 – Stockton*

FOOD & DRINK

It is said that there are so many restaurants in San Francisco that it would be possible for everybody living there to go out at the same time and still find a place to eat. It is also said that nowhere in the USA are people so careful about staying slim and healthy than in California.

How can you reconcile these two things? It is only possible if the food is really good. The gastronomy in North California is the most refined and easy on the stomach in America – and the main strongholds are Napa Valley and San Francisco. However; for decades even this cuisine suffered from a minority complex and the chefs merely copied what they had seen in Europe. But

then, they discovered Californian cuisine. The foundations: cook light, vary the ethnic specialities of the many peoples in the country, and use produce fresh from local markets. Parallel to this, winegrowers in nearby Napa Valley also changed their methods and moved away from mass-produced to high-quality wines. These two basics – wonderful wines and fresh, local products – are also the fundamentals of outstanding regional cooking elsewhere. There is something else that makes a culinary pilgrimage to San Francisco worthwhile: the great variety of national dishes. Japanese, Chinese, Russian, German, Italian, Creole, Indian – these can all be

Photo: Pizza and more – in Calzone's Restaurant

In San Francisco, you will discover dishes from all around the world – and you can eat in a 'different country' every day

found next to each other. And, in a city with more than 1000 restaurants, you can be certain that if it's no good, it will not be open long.

One of the rules in American restaurants is that guests cannot choose to sit where they want; the service staff will show you to your place. Tips and taxes are not included in the price. The waiters and waitresses usually receive no – or only a very

small – salary and a tip of 15 to 20 percent of the net bill is appropriate.

COFFEE, BRUNCH & ICE CREAM

INSIDER TIP **AXIS CAFÉ** (131 D2) *(ⁿⁿ Q9)*
This is the place on Potrero Hill where art students, designers and university lecturer meet over a caffè latte and a salad.

Good coffee and frequent live music in the legendary artists' meeting place – Caffe Trieste

A fireplace provides warmth on foggy days. And, in contrast to other restaurants, nobody will chase you off of the large sheltered terrace after your meal. If you have a student ID, you will be given a ten percent discount. *Daily | 1201 8th St./corner of 16th St. | Muni 19 – Polk*

LA BOULANGE (124 B3) *(⑳ N3)*

Freshly baked goods several times a day, delicious sandwiches and salads – this attracts the residents of Russian Hill on sunny days. *Daily | 2310 Polk St. | Muni 19 – Polk*

INSIDER TIP CAFFE TRIESTE
(124 C2) *(⑳ P3)*

You will breathe in history in this café in North Beach: the walls are covered with photos of writers who philosophised over the meaning of life here. Kerouac, Ginsberg, Snyder – many of the heroes of the beat generation sat in this time-honoured coffee house. *Daily | 609 Vallejo St. | Muni 45 – Union/Stockton*

INSIDER TIP COFFEE ADVENTURES
(124 B1) *(⑳ N2)*

Bob and Nicole Beggs fulfilled their dream of having their own small café – only a stone's throw away from the Cannery. They serve the best *chai tea latte* in town, bagel specialities and *iced coffee*. There are changing exhibitions of works by photographers and other artists. *Daily | 1331 Columbus Ave. | Muni F – Market*

THE CRÊPE HOUSE ● (124 B3) *(⑳ N4)*

Enormous servings of exquisite omelettes, delicious crêpes and waffles and the perfect place to watch the locals. On clear days, the sun lights up the tables on the pavement and street – for which some parking spaces had to be sacrificed. *Daily | 1755 Polk St. | Muni 19 – Polk*

HUMPHRY SLOCOMBE ICE CREAM ☺
(130 C4) *(⑳ O11)*

There are often crowds queuing up in front of this organic ice-cream parlour. Every day around a dozen of the total of 82 weird-and-wonderful flavours such *as Jesus Juice, Butter Beer* and *Guinness Gingerbread* are freshly prepared. *Daily | 2790 Harrison St. | Muni 27 – Bryant*

MARIO'S BOHEMIAN CIGAR STORE AND CAFÉ (124 C2) (*Ⓜ P3*)

This small, cosy corner café on Washington Square is always well visited. Try the grilled *focaccia. Daily | 566 Columbus Ave. | Muni 30 – Stockton*

INSIDER TIP RED'S JAVA HOUSE ⋏ (125 E4) (*Ⓜ S5*)

This piece of contemporary history has been open since 1923. There is much more than coffee here where dock workers used to warm up. Banker and Giants' fans enjoy reasonably priced hamburgers and fish & chips with a view of the Bay; on warm days, outside. *Daily | Pier 30 | Muni N – Judah*

ST. FRANCIS FOUNTAIN (125 E4) (*Ⓜ P11*)

Probably the oldest diner in San Francisco has been in the business since 1918: feel-good breakfast *(chocolate chip pancakes!)*, great ice-cream sundaes and wonderful milkshakes. And a bar laden down with sweet treats. *Daily | 2810 24th St. | Muni 27 – Bryant*

INSIDER TIP SWENSEN'S ICE CREAM ● (124 B2) (*Ⓜ N3*)

In 1948, Earle Swensen opened this ice-cream parlour and it became a worldwide hit with its fame even reaching Asia and the Middle East. The brave risk eating the *Bubble Gum* and *Wild at Heart* creations; the less adventurous stick to *Wild Mountain Blackberry* and *Turkish Coffee*. Only three blocks away from Lombard St. *Daily | 1999 Hyde St. | tel. 775 68 18 | Cable Car PH – Powell Hyde*

RESTAURANTS: EXPENSIVE

ACQUERELLO (124 B4) (*Ⓜ N4*)

Suzette Gresham-Tognetti serves amazing pasta and fish specialities and Giancarlo Paterlini makes certain that they are accompanied by the right wine. The waiters

---

MARCO POLO HIGHLIGHTS

★ **Bix**
A journey through time back to the 1930s
→ p. 64

★ **Gary Danko**
The most famous restaurant in San Francisco
→ p. 64

★ **Blowfish Sushi**
Creative high-end sushi
→ p. 64

★ **Greens**
The non-plus-ultra for vegetarians → p. 65

★ **House of Prime Rib**
Nomen est omen: the home of probably the best steaks in town → p. 65

★ **1300 on Fillmore**
Soul food with live jazz and the unique Gospel Brunch every Sunday → p. 65

★ **NOPA**
So good that even chefs come here after work to eat and drink → p. 67

★ **Zuni Café**
Meeting place for the 'in' crowd and one of the best recommendations for a delicious lunch → p. 69

★ **In-N-Out Burger**
Hamburgers and milkshakes, all freshly made, close to Fisherman's Wharf → p. 70

★ **Pluto's**
Salads made to order – with meat if you want it → p. 71

in what was once a chapel seem to know what guests want before they do, without ever being pushy or stand-offish. *Closed Sun/Mon | 1722 Sacramento St. | tel. 5 67 54 32 | Muni 1 – California*

BIX ★ (125 D3) (𝄞 P4)

Exclusive and cool at the same time. With its art-déco furnishings and live jazz, this is a hidden, romantic gem in the city's Financial District. Get dressed for it! The restaurant is almost like the dining room on a cruise ship from the period. Reserve in advance! *Daily from 5.30pm, Fri from 11.30am | 56 Gold St. | tel. 4 33 63 00 | Muni 10 – Townsend*

BLOWFISH SUSHI ★ (130 C2) (𝄞 P10)

With its exhibition of Manga comics on the dark red walls, this restaurant creates a cool Japanese feeling. Sushi chef Ritsuo

GOURMET RESTAURANTS

Fleur de Lys (124 C4) (𝄞 O5)

Star chef Hubert Keller really has his hands full. He has opened two new restaurants in Las Vegas and reveals the secrets of his fabulous cooking on television. From $72, *closed at lunchtime and on Sun | 777 Sutter St. | tel. 6 73 77 79 | Cable Car C – California*

Gary Danko ★ (124 B1) (𝄞 N2)

If you are looking for a peaceful and romantic restaurant, you should let yourself be pampered by Gary Danko. His restaurant serves superb French cuisine and is considered the best in town. From $68. *Closed at lunchtime | 800 North Point St. | tel. 7 49 20 60 | Muni Cable Car PH – Powell & Hyde*

Masa's (124 C4) (𝄞 P5)

This is one of the best French restaurants – with a Californian touch. The wildfowl are really outstanding. Vintage French and Californian wine – you will only find a better selection in Napa Valley. Jacket required, tie optional. Book in advance! From $95. *Closed at lunchtime and Sun/Mon | 648 Bush St. | tel. 9 89 71 54 | Cable Car PH – Powell & Hyde*

Michael Mina (125 D3) (𝄞 Q4)

The star chef who was born in Egypt now has 18 restaurants in the USA, four of them in San Francisco. He returned to his roots at the first place he worked – the former Aqua – which he simply renamed Michael Mina. Here, you can either choose the chef's tasting menu ($115) or order à la carte. *Tip: Maine Lobster Pot Pie* (market price). *Daily | 252 California St. | tel. 397-9222 | Cable Car C – California*

One Market (125 E3) (𝄞 R4)

This restaurant is somewhat overlooked by many gourmets although its head chef Mark Dommen mixes local products with the art of French cuisine – something he learned from his mentor Hubert Keller in the *Fleur de Lys*. For $85, you can experience a six-course meal at the chef's table, with personal service, as part of a 'behind the scenes' tour of the kitchen. Excellent steak and fish dishes and a varied wine list. *Daily | 1 Market St: | tel. 7 77 55 77 | Muni F – Market*

Kuleto's: an institution for all gourmets near Union Square

Tsuchida is the first cook in San Francisco to be given permission by the health authorities to cook the restaurant's name giver, the blowfish. You can watch the artistic preparation of the various dishes at the Sushi Bar. *Sat/Sun closed at lunchtime | 2170 Bryant St. | tel. 2 85 38 48 | Muni 27 – Bryant*

GREENS ★ ☼ (112 A1) (*M2*)

This restaurant in Fort Mason, located on a pier jutting out into San Francisco Bay, is one of the top addresses for meatless dishes. The view of the Golden Gate Bridge and the dazzling red of the sunset will make your watercress salad and grilled vegetables taste even better. *Closed Mon lunchtime, Sun evening | Fort Mason, Building A | tel. 7 71 62 22 | Muni 30 – Stockton*

HOUSE OF PRIME RIB ★
(124 B3) (*N4*)

In what is probably the best steakhouse in town, the 21-day-air-dried meat is carved at your table just the way you like

it. Try the *English cut* and *creamed spinach*. Fabulous cocktails, but: bookings are essential! *Closed lunchtime | 1906 Van Ness Ave. | tel. 8 85 46 05 | Muni 1 – California*

KULETO'S (124 C4) (*P5*)

A marble floor, high ceilings and a *Brunswick bar* brought over to San Francisco by a sailing ship at the end of the 19th century – the atmosphere is typical of Old England but the food served is a mix of Italian and Californian cuisine. *Daily | 221 Powell St. | tel. 3 97 77 20 | Cable Car – Powell & Hyde, Powell & Mason*

RESTAURANTS: MODERATE

1300 ON FILLMORE ★
(123 E5) (*M6*)

A modern supper club with a chic atmosphere: head chef David Lawrence mixes his English heritage with traces of Jamaica, France and the southern states of the USA. Try his *catfish* and *cornbread*. Live jazz on Friday evenings; a fabulous gospel brunch at 11am and 1pm on Sundays. *Daily | 1300*

Fillmore St. | tel. 7 71 71 00 | Muni 38 – Geary

ALEGRÍAS (124 B2) (*M L3*)

The food and interior decoration – wine-red chairs, stucco and pottery – is as Spanish as it gets. The owner and head chef Faedi González is proud of his heritage and cooks using recipes handed down by his mother and grandmother. And that is just what the Latinos love. *Closed lunchtime | 2018 Lombard St. | tel. 9 29 88 88 | Muni 30 – Stockton*

ent films while you enjoy the Californian cuisine prepared by Gayle Pirie and her husband John in the inner courtyard. *Daily in the evening, Sat/Sun from noon | 2534 Mission St. | tel. 6 48 76 00 | Muni 14 – Mission*

INDIAN OVEN (129 E1) (*M M8*)

There is not very much room in this popular Indian restaurant in Lower Haight. The *Tandoori chicken*, marinated in yoghurt and spices and baked in a clay oven, is always a hit. *Daily | 233 Fillmore St. | tel.*

The cooks and guests make sure that everything is freshly prepared in the Swan Oyster Depot

FRESCA (123 E4) (*M L5*)

Julio Calvo-Perez and his wife Zoila come from Lima and serve Peruvian dishes inspired by Julio's grandmother in their restaurant. Order *lomo saltado* (thinly sliced, stir-fired beef) or *ceviche mixto* (marinated seafood) with a carafe of sangria to wash it down. *Daily | 2114 Fillmore St. | tel. 4 47 26 68 | Muni 1 – California*

FOREIGN CINEMA (130 B4) (*M N10*)

The name gives it away – you can watch cinema classics and the latest independ-

6 26 16 28 | Muni 5 – Fulton, 71 – Haight/ Noriega

JOHN'S GRILL (124 C4–5) (*M P6*)

This restaurant that opened in 1908 is a must for all fans of Dashiell Hammett and his private detective character Sam Spade. The author came here frequently in the 1920s and the lamps, wood and leather have all been preserved the way Hammett/ Spade found them. *Daily | 63 Ellis St. | tel. 9 86 00 69 | Cable Car PH – Powell & Hyde, PM – Powell & Mason*

NEW ASIA ● (124 C3) (*ᗐ P4*)
As authentic as it gets: not only Chinese clans enjoy filling themselves up on the delicious dim-sums in this cavernous Restaurant. *Daily | 772 Pacific Ave. | tel. 3 9166 66 | Muni 30 – Stockton*

NOPA ★ ☺ (123 E6) (*ᗐ L7*)
This is where the city's cooks and other restaurant staff get together after they finish work – the kitchen serves novel, organic-food creations until 1 o'clock in the morning. Delicious! *Daily | 560 Divisadero St. | tel. 8 64 86 43 | Muni 21 – Hayes*

THE POT STICKER (124 C3) (*ᗐ P4*)
Why visit the tourist traps in Chinatown when there are restaurants like this one? For starters, try pancakes and the traditional pot stickers – Chinese wontons stuffed with meat or vegetables. *Daily | 150 Waverly Place | tel. 3 97 99 85 | Muni 1 – California*

SPORK (130 B4) (*ᗐ N10*)
Spork: a combination of spoon and fork is the standard piece of cutlery used in the Kentucky Fried Chicken chain that used to be here. Today, the smartened-up diner serves new American cuisine – you must try the rosemary bread! *Valencia St. | tel. 6 43 50 00 | Muni 14 – Mission*

SWAN OYSTER DEPOT
(124 B4) (*ᗐ N5*)
Oysters, crab chowder and smoked salmon: Swan Oyster Depot serves INSIDER TIP all of San Francisco's fish specialities – freshly caught and at fair prices. Don't expect any kind of luxury; you eat at rustic counters. It is jam-packed at lunchtime but is always a unique experience for lovers of fish and seafood! *Closed Sun | 1517 Polk St. | tel. 6 73 11 01 | Muni 1 – California*

TADICH GRILL (125 D3) (*ᗐ Q4*)
You will feel like you are an extra in a classic film noir as soon as you walk through the door of the oldest restaurant in California. Outstanding fish dishes; try the cioppino stew. No reservations. *Closed Sun | 240 California St. | tel. 3 9118 49 | Muni Cable Car C – California*

INSIDER TIP ▶ THAI SPICE
(124 B3) (*ᗐ N4*)
A laid-back Thai restaurant without blasting music and dim lighting – what a relief! We recommend *tom ka* as a starter followed by *green* or *pumpkin yellow curry* and *sweet sticky rice with mango* for dessert. The best *Thai ice tea* in town. *Daily | 1730 Polk St. | tel. 7 75 47 77 | Muni 1 – California*

LOW BUDGET

▶ *Phat Philly* ☺ (130 B4) (*ᗐ N11*): Why go to Philadelphia when you can choose between 15 *Philly Cheesesteaks* in San Francisco? Beef, raised naturally, never frozen, fresh every day. Try the *California Cheesesteak!* *Daily | 3388 24th St. | Muni 14 – Mission*

▶ A dozen dim sum specialities after midnight? You can order a Chinese lunch all day long in the *Dim Sum Bar* (124 B4) (*ᗐ O5*) – and it's not expensive either! *Daily | 620 O'Farrell St. | Muni 38 – Geary*

▶ *Big Nate's BBQ* (130 B2) (*ᗐ O8*): here, the chef Nat Thurmond, a former Golden State Warriors' basketball star, grills personally. Enormous servings and the meat melts in your mouth. *Daily | 1665 Folsom St. | Muni 12 – Folsom/Pacific*

LOCAL SPECIALITIES

For those who are unfamiliar with what the names of certain dishes mean, here are some items found in San Francisco's pubs, cafés and restaurants that visitors from other parts of the English-speaking world may find puzzling.

▶ **baked potato** – often served with sour cream

▶ **burrito** – beans, rice, chicken or meat, wrapped in a tortilla (photo left). The deluxe version also has avocado, sour cream and cheese. Now, it is even possible to buy San Francisco-style burritos in New York

▶ **chowder** – creamy soup: especially, *clam chowder* is one of the city's specialities

▶ **crabs** – Fisherman's Wharf and Ghirardelli square are the best places to buy delicious, freshly caught, crabs

▶ **crab cakes** – don't be confused by the name; these cakes – made of crabmeat, onions, chilli, herbs and breadcrumbs – are not small but about the size of a hamburger

▶ **dim sum** – each dim sum is stuffed with a different mixture raging from crabmeat, vegetables and meat to more exotic fillings

▶ **eggs sunny side up with bacon and hash browns** – breakfast classic

▶ **hangtown fry** – a speciality from the Gold Rush days: a rich omelette with oysters and bacon

▶ **pumpkin pie** – you will find enormous pumpkins – green, yellow, orange, as well as some with stripes – in every grocery shop in summer and autumn. It is no wonder that *pumpkin pie* is one of San Franciscans' favourite desserts (photo right)

▶ **roast turkey** – served with mashed potatoes and sweet potatoes: the classic Thanksgiving meal

▶ **sourdough bread** – crispy and delicious. Isidore Boudin opened his bakery in 1849; more than 150 years later *San Francisco sourdough bread* is popular everywhere in the USA

YANK SING (125 D4) *(𝄞 R4)*
If you're craving for the best dim sums in San Francisco, don't head for Chinatown but the Downtown area instead. *Daily | 101 Spear St. | tel. 9 57 93 00 | Muni F – Market*

ZUNI CAFÉ ⭐ (129 F2) (*🛇 N7*)

Artists, politicians, real celebrities and wannabes meet in Judy Rogers' trendy café. There is a different menu every day, the wine selection is outstanding, the atmosphere lively but relaxed. *Closed Mon | 1658 Market St. | tel. 5 52 25 22 | Muni F – Market*

RESTAURANTS: BUDGET

INSIDERTIP ▶ BALADIE GOURMET CAFÉ (125 D4) (*🛇 P5*)

Here, in the heart of the Financial District, Mike and Nick Bazlamit prepare enormous, inexpensive, Arabian schawarma and Greek gyros filled with chicken, lamb and beef, hummus and tsatsiki. They also serve delicious, freshly-made salads. *Closed Sun | 337 Kearny St. | tel. 9 89 66 29 | Muni F – Market*

CAFÉ CHAAT (125 D5) (*🛇 Q6*)

You will be bowled over by the size of the servings in this Indian-Pakistani restaurant. Start your meal with a *chicken tikka masala wrap.* Daily | *320 3rd St. | tel. 9 79 99 46 | Muni 30 – Stockton*

CALZONE'S (124 C2–3) (*🛇 P3*)

This is the place to enjoy pizza, pasta and salads in a lively atmosphere and with a wonderful view of all that is going on at North Beach – if the weather is fine, tables are put out in front of the restaurant. *Daily | 430 Columbus Ave. | tel. 3 97 36 00 | Muni 30 – Stockton*

CONNECTICUT YANKEE (131 D2–3) (*🛇 Q9*)

This really welcoming restaurant, which has been open since 1907, is run by two Boston Red Sox fans. There are baseball items on the walls and a television where sometimes football games are shown. Sunny beer garden in the inner courtyard. You should really try the sugar-coated fries with garlic sauce. *Daily | 100 Connecticut St. | tel. 5 52 44 40 | Muni 10 – Townsend*

New paths to rehabilitation: Delancey Street Restaurant

DELANCEY STREET RESTAURANT ☖ ☺ (125 E5) (*🛇 R6*)

A wide variety of well-prepared American food with a view of the Bay. The restaurant is run by the *Delancey Street Foundation* that makes it possible for former prisoners to start life anew. *Daily | 600 Embarcadero St. | tel. 5 12 51 79 | Muni N – Judah*

INSIDERTIP ▶ GRUBSTAKE (124 B4) (*🛇 N5*)

Only in San Francisco: the Santos family serves burgers, steaks and Portuguese specialities in a railway carriage that is at least 90 years old. *Closed Mon–Fri lunchtime | 1525 Pine St. | tel. 6 73 82 68 | Muni 109 – Polk*

IN-N-OUT BURGER ★ ☺
(124 B1) (*𝄞 N2*)

This Californian family business is older than McDonald's and has opened exactly 258 offshoots in three USA states since 1948. You can only eat hamburgers, *French fries* and milkshakes, but they are all made on the premises using fresh products – there are no freezers or microwaves. And, you can really taste the difference. *Daily until 1am | 333 Jefferson St. | Muni F – Market*

JOHN'S SNACK AND DELI
(125 D4) (*𝄞 Q5*)

John Park and his mother, Sang Sook Park, give a taste of Korea to dishes from all over the world, as well as preparing traditional food such as *bi bim bop* – mmm, tasty! *Closed Sat/Sun | 40 Battery St. | tel. 4 34 46 34 | Muni F – Market*

INSIDER TIP KING LING
(124 B4) (*𝄞 O5*)

A likeable, laid-back couple run this miniature Chinese restaurant in the Downtown area. Unbeatable, delicious lunchtime special: *sweet & sour soup* and a main course for $5.75. The sesame chicken and crispy beef are also outstanding. *Closed Sun | 643 Geary St. | tel. 5 67 18 88 | Muni 38 – Geary*

INSIDER TIP KITCHENETTE
(131 E3) (*𝄞 S10*)

'Spontaneous organic covert nourishment' is how the cooks describe the freshly-prepared sandwiches they sell from a garage door in the Dogpatch district. They all used to work in the best restaurants in town – and you can taste it. You can find out about the daily specials on their website (*www.kitchenettesf.com*). Come early! *Mon–Fri 11.30am–1.30pm or until they run out! | 958 Illinois St. | Muni T – Third*

MAMA'S (124 C2) (*𝄞 P3*)

No matter how long they have queue – this is where the locals come to enjoy delicious omelettes and *French toast*. *Tue–Sun 8am–3pm | 1701 Stockton St. | tel. 3 62 64 21 | Muni 30 – Stockton*

MEL'S DRIVE-IN (122 A5) (*𝄞 L3*)

The best place in San Francisco to enjoy an 'honest burger' in classic surroundings is Mel's Drive-in. Lime-green leather seats and simple tables with lots of chrome bring back the feeling of the 1960s. There are four offshoots and the one on Lombard Street is especially recommendable. *Daily 6am–1am, Sat/Sun open 24 hours | 2165 Lombard St. | tel. 9 21 28 67 | Muni 76 – Marin Headlands*

STREET FOOD AROUND THE CLOCK

Mobile cooks make sure the city does not starve. It all started with the *Tamale Lady* with her cool box full of home-made specialities who was awaited eagerly in the bars of the Mission district. She was followed by professionals and amateurs, the internet and the recession. Today, there are several dozen *food carts* and *pop-up restaurants* out and about in San Francisco. When they are mobile, they announce their present location per twitter (*www. twitter.com*) or on the web. Some of the best are Ken Ken Ramen (@KenKen Ramen, Japanese), Liba falafel (@liba falafel, Mediterranean), Spencer on the Go (@chezspencergo, French), Da Beef (*www.dabeef.com*, Chicago hotdogs) and Little Skillet (*www.littleskilletsf.com*, Southern food).

Mel's Drive-in was the location of the film classic 'American Graffiti'

OSHA THAI (129 E1) (🛱 O5)

Where to go after bars close at 2am? To the first of the seven Oshai Thais in the city that is open until 3am on Fridays and Saturdays: quick, tasty, spicy. *Daily | 696 Geary St. | tel. 6 73 23 68 | Muni 68 – Geary*

PANCHO VILLA (130 B2) (🛱 N9)

There is a *taquería* on every corner of the Mexican Mission district. Is there any thing less expensive, but more nourishing, than a burrito with rice, vegetables and meat? This is the best place to go for the finest and biggest *burritos, quesadillas* and *tacos*. *Daily | 3071 16th St. | tel. 8 64 88 40 | Muni 14 – Mission*

PLUTO'S ★ (123 D2) (🛱 K3)

He who hesitates here is lost. In Pluto's the chefs whip up a salad just the way you want it from two dozen different ingredients – going as far as tasty strips of steak – in almost no time. Their slogan is 'fresh food for a hungry universe'. *Daily | 3285 Scott St. | tel. 7 75 88 67 | Muni 30 – Stockton*

INSIDER TIP ▶ SAIGON SANDWICHES (124 B5) (🛱 O6)

The Little Saigon district is where you can feel the heartbeat of San Francisco's Vietnamese community. When you first look into the dimly-lit shop you will find it hard to believe that they make the best *banh mi* (Vietnamese sandwiches) in town. But the two ladies prepare wonderfully spicy food for a mere $3. Our favourite: pork meatball. No credit cards. *Daily | 560 Larkin St. | tel. 474 56 98 | Muni 19 – Polk*

INSIDER TIP ▶ SALLY'S (131 D2) (🛱 Q9)

The ABC and SMS omelettes made by the, always cheerful, owner Stuart Bai are pure bliss, the blueberry banana smoothie is full of vitamins. *Daily | 300 De Haro St. | tel. 6 26 60 60 | Muni 19 – Polk*

SHOPPING

San Francisco is much more a city of small and large shops than department stores, although there are some luxurious ones, and many designers from Milan and Paris have boutiques in the city.

European prêt-à-porter fashion still sets the style and you will also be able to find many elegant, chic clothes made in America. The boutiques of the top national and international labels are grouped around Union Square, while you will find less expensive souvenirs and T-shirts in Chinatown.

For Americans, shopping is much more than just buying things, it is a way of life. And this applies especially to San Franciscans. You probably know just how bored many of the sales people in European shops seem, or how groceries are scanned

WHERE TO START?

The **Westfield Centre** on Market Street **(122 C5)** *(Ⴚ P6)*, with more than 150 shops, cafés, restaurants and a cinema, is a real Mecca for shoppers. Easy to reach: almost all Muni trams, Bart trains in the city area, numerous buses and the PH/PM Powel& Hyde/Mason cable cars stop just a short distance away.

Photo: In the heart of Chinatown

Looking for the fashion trends of yesterday, today and tomorrow? You will find them all here!

at the cash desk without any attention being paid.

You won't find any of this impoliteness and lack of interest in San Francisco. There, the customer is still treated as what he or she should be: a king! – and your purchases will always be packed for you; and that not only in supermarkets.

But, with all the joy of shopping, you should not overlook the fact that value-added tax (currently 9.5 percent) is always added to the ticketed price. And, don't forget to ask if the new electric toy will also function when you take it back to your home country.

Most shops are open every day; some chemists and supermarkets never close. You can shop at most of the department stores, medium and small boutiques from 10am to 8pm.

ANTIQUES

ANTIQUES

ANTONIO'S ANTIQUES
(125 D6) *(ᗰ Q7)*
Here, you will find antiques from all over the world. *701 Bryant St. | Muni 27 – Bryant*

of classical and philosophical works, poetry and English-language editions of literature from the Third World. There are also readings by new writers and other literary events. *261 Columbus Ave. | www.citylights.com | Muni 30 – Stockton*

City Lights Bookstore: a bookshop and world-famous writers' meeting place

ARIA ANTIQUES (124 C2) *(ᗰ P3)*
Bill Haskell's mixture of gallery and museum has a great selection of glass eyes, anatomical models, wooden toys, old maps, globes, letters and engravings. *1522 Grant Ave. | Muni 30 – Stockton*

BOOKS & MAPS

CITY LIGHT BOOKSTORE ★
(124 C3) *(ᗰ P4)*
The bookshop run by the author and independent publisher Lawrence Ferlinghetti has become a legend. A unique selection

INSIDER TIP ▶ GREEN APPLE BOOKS
(122 B5) *(ᗰ G6)*
Gigantic stock of new and second-hand books. The relaxed atmosphere will make you want to browse for hours. *506 Clement St. | Muni 1 – California*

SIERRA CLUB BOOKSTORE
(125 D4) *(ᗰ Q5)*
Tourists and hikers will find all the information on the surroundings of San Francisco, the Grand Canyon and other national parks in this bookshop. *85 2nd St. | Muni 14 – Mission*

OFFICE SUPPLIES

PATRICK & COMPANY
(125 D4) (𝄞 O7)

Now that *Waldeck's* has closed, this is one of the few remaining independent office supply dealers – and it has been that since 1873! All of you wishes – from drawing pins to designer chairs, from lead pencils to de luxe fountain pens – will be fulfilled here. *560 Market St. | Muni F – Market*

COMPUTERS

APPLE STORE
(124 C4) (𝄞 P5)

Here, you will not only be able to try out all the latest Macs and iPods, but also take part in workshops and check your e-mails. *Stockton St. | Muni F – Market*

BEST BUY
(130 C2) (𝄞 O8)

Audio, video, mobile phone and PC accessories, CDs and DVDs, software, PC and video games and much, much more. *1717 Harrison St. | Muni 47 – Van Ness*

CENTRAL COMPUTER SYSTEMS
(124 C5) (𝄞 P6)

PCs, laptops, individual components – this shop, which smells of solder, has the best prices. *837 Howard St. | Muni 30 – Stockton*

DRUGSTORE

WALGREENS ★
(125 D4) (𝄞 N7)

Following the demise of *RiteAid*, Walgreens now dominates the market with more than 70 shops selling cosmetics from soap to perfume, medicines and drinks. Some even sell alcohol. *730 Market St. | Muni F – Market*

GIFTS & SOUVENIRS

CHINATOWN KITE SHOP
(124 C3) (𝄞 P4)

Can anything be more uplifting than flying a kite at Ocean Beach or Crissy Field? This shop has the finest selection of conventional and Asian kites. *717 Grant St. | Muni 1 – California*

INSIDER TIP ▶ NATIONAL PARK STORE AT PIER 39 (124 C1) (𝄞 N2)

Souvenirs that your friends and family will really like: bags and cups with motifs by the artists Paul Madonna and Michael

---

MARCO POLO HIGHLIGHTS

★ **City Lights Bookstore**
This combination of bookshop and publishing house released Allen Ginsburg's poem 'Howl' in 1956 → p. 74

★ **Walgreens**
American drugstore with reasonable prices → p. 75

★ **Neiman-Marcus**
Revel in the luxury of a consumer's paradise → p. 76

★ **Pier 39**
Hustle and bustle at the harbour with shops, restaurants and even sea lions → p. 77

★ **Westfield Centre**
The epicentre of shopping: fashion and food to suit every budget → p. 77

★ **Original Levi's Store**
The ancestral seat of Levi's jeans → p. 79

ful prints, books and Alcatraz
Pier 39 | Muni F – Market

HEALTH & COSMETICS

BOBBI BROWN COSMETICS AT BLOOMINGDALE'S (124 C5) (🛱 P6)

The make-up created by the lady from New York, Bobbi Brown, aims at a natural look, unlike the artificial appearance achieved by many of her competitors. The success of the cosmetic series she still supervises so scrupulously shows that she is right. Reserved sales assistants. *845 Market St. | Muni F – Market*

LOW BUDGET

▶ If you manage to survive the chaos of *Ross Dress for Less* (124 C5) (🛱 P5), you will be rewarded with real bargains – the shop offers brands such as Calvin Klein, Polo and Hilfiger at dumping prices. *799 Market St. | Muni F – Market*

▶ The *DSW Shoe Warehouse* (124 C4) (🛱 P5) sells designer shoes – for both men and women – at low prices. The variety of models often compensates for sometimes limited range of sizes. *111 Powell St. | Muni cable car PH – Powell & Hyde*

▶ *Out of the Closet* (124 B4) (🛱 N5) is a cool second-hand clothing chain run by the Aids Healthcare Foundation. *1498 Polk St. | Cable Car C – California*

▶ *Trader Joe's* (130 C2) (🛱 O2) is a spacious supermarket owned by the Albrecht family of Aldi fame. *401 Bay St. | Muni F – Market*

GENERAL NUTRITION CENTER (124 C4) (🛱 Q5)

Heaven for the health-conscious: 2000 varieties of vitamins, herbal mixtures, sports foods and diet pills. *576 Market St. | Muni F – Market*

RAINBOW GROCERY ☺ (130 B1) (🛱 O8)

The Rainbow only sells organic products and cosmetics. If that's what you're looking for, you can be sure to find it here. *1745 Folsom St. | Muni 9 – San Bruno*

DEPARTMENT STORES

CANTON BAZAAR (124 C3–4) (🛱 P4)

Three floors full of kitsch, practical things, souvenirs and genuine oriental art in the heart of Chinatown. *616 Grant Ave. | Muni 1 – California*

MACY'S (124 C4) (🛱 P5)

The local branch of the famous New York department store is the seven-floor epitome of a spending spree. Here, each brand has its own section and you will really be able to shop till you drop! *170 O'Farrell St. | Muni 30 – Stockton*

NEIMAN-MARCUS ★ (124 C4) (🛱 P5)

This elegant department store is worth visiting even if you don't buy anything. The rotunda and glazed gallery were eye-catchers 100 years ago when the former shop *City of Paris* opened its doors. Not cheap, but unquestionably the best service in town – in all departments. *150 Stockton St. | Muni 30 – Stockton*

MALLS

Most of these malls have one or two department stores, countless boutiques and often cinemas and restaurants.

THE CANNERY (124 B1) (*☐ N2*)

This used to be the biggest peach tinning factory in the world. Today, the shops here – and in the Anchorage Center one block away – are struggling to survive; at least there are still bars, cafés and live music. *2801 Leavenworth St. | Muni F – Market*

CROCKER GALLERIA (124 C4) (*☐ Q5*)

This mall is modelled on the Galleria Vittorio Emmanuele in Milan and caters to shoppers with plenty of money to spare. *50 Post St., near Union Square | Muni F – Market*

EMBARCADERO CENTER (125 D3) (*☐ Q4*)

In the heart of the downtown district with a cinema, more than 70 restaurants and shops, as well as an ice-skating rink in winter. *1 Embarcadero Center | Muni 1 – California*

GHIRARDELLI SQUARE (124 A1) (*☐ N2*)

The Ghirardelli family's former chocolate factory has also now developed into an open-air mall with lots of entertainment. *900 North Point St. | Muni 19 – Polk*

JAPAN CENTER (124 A4) (*☐ M5–6*)

Strange but true: The Japan Center is what it claims to be. Everything here is Japanese – from the hotel to the shiatsu massage centre. *Corner of Post and Buchanan St. | Muni 38 – Geary*

INSIDER TIP ▶ NEW PEOPLE (123 E4) (*☐ M5*)

The newest attraction in Japantown is an amazingly clean, four-storey shopping centre with a café, anime cinema, art gallery and shops. The largest is completely uninhibited in celebrating Japanese pop culture with music, books, DVDs and toys; four smaller ones offer Gothic, Lolita and

Shopping Japanese style: New People Mall

pretty *Kawaiian* clothes. *1746 Post St. | Muni 2 – Clement*

PIER 39 ★ (124 C1) (*☐ O–P1*)

Fishermen steer clear of the tourist epicentre on the harbour of San Francisco if they can. But not those who like wild sea lions, an aquarium, a merry-go-round, countless boutiques, restaurants and cafés along with the unavoidable kitsch. *2 Beach St. | Muni F – Market*

^IWESTFIELD CENTRE ★ ● (124 C5) (*☐ P6*)

The more than 150 small and large shops, restaurants and cinemas will make an all-out attack on your credit card. This temple to commerce, where you will really find everything from cosmetics, books and technical items to groceries is crowned with a glass dome and spiral escalators. *865 Market St. | Muni F – Market*

the prices for fruit and vegetables are much lower and the selection is just as large. *Wed 7am–5pm, Sun 8am–5pm | 1182 Market St. | Muni F – Market*

Plants, fruit and vegetables: everything is fresh at Ferry Plaza Farmer's Market

MARKETS

INSIDER TIP ▶ FERRY PLAZA FARMER'S MARKET ⊙ (125 D2) (*∭ R4*)

This is where you will find all of the regional products that make Californian cuisine so wonderful. The chefs of the best eateries shop here and many of them have snack bars where you can get in the right mood for the culinary delights waiting for you in their restaurants. *Sat 8am–2pm, Tue/Thu 10am–2pm, at other times during the season | One Ferry Building | Muni F – Market*

HEART OF THE CITY FARMER'S MARKET ● ⊙ (124 B5) (*∭ O7*)

The location is not as picturesque as the Farmer's Market in the Ferry Building but

FASHION & ACCESSORIES

ABERCROMBIE & FITCH (124 C5) (*∭ P6*)

The shop for hiking clothes that was established in New York in 1892 has developed into one of the most popular fashion chains where the 15-to-35-year-old crowd fight for the cool, sporty jeans, sweatshirts, college jackets and skirts. *865 Market St. | Muni F – Market*

BANANA REPUBLIC (124 C4) (*∭ P5*)

Fashion that is relaxed and casual but still suitable for wearing to the office. Here, you will find everything you have been looking for – made of linen, gossamer silk or tough denim. *256 Grant Ave. | Muni 30 – Stockton*

GAP (125 C5) (*M P6*)

Another San Francisco original: Don Fisher could not find any jeans that really fit him and so he and his wife Doris opened their own shop called Gap in 1969: laid-back fashion for all age groups. *890 Market St. | Muni F – Market*

NIKETOWN (124 C4) (*M P5*)

The name says it all: this is where can buy everything produced by Nike – as long as your money holds out. *278 Post St. | Muni 30 – Stockton*

ORIGINAL LEVI'S STORE ★ (124 C4) (*M P5*)

Levis' answer to Niketown just down the street: a four-storey shop full of jeans, invented by Löb Strauss whose firm Levi Strauss & Co. started producing them for San Francisco's gold diggers in 1853. *300 Post St. | Muni 30 – Stockton*

REI 😊 (125 D6) (*M P8*)

An El Dorado for hikers, climbers, skiers, cyclists and campers. In 1938, 23 mountaineers founded the first REI; today, the cooperative (owned by the staff and clients) has more than 80 shops and encourages a responsible attitude towards nature. *840 Brennan St. | Muni 27 Bryant*

INSIDER TIP TIMBUK2 (124 A6) (*M N7*)

Expensive but good: messengers and the 'in' crowd have been underway with bags from Timbuk2 since 1989. *506 Hayes St. | Muni 21 – Hayes*

MUSIC

AMOEBA MUSIC (128 C2) (*M J8*)

The second shop of the record label established in Berkeley in 1990 housed in an old bowling alley. An incredible stock of new and second-hand CDs, DVDs, laser discs and vinyl records, as well as free concerts by local stars of tomorrow. *1855 Haight St. | Muni 7 – Haight, 71 – Haight-Noriega*

GROOVE MERCHANT RECORDS (129 E1) (*M J8*)

This is the place to find those rare jazz, disco, soul, reggae, hip-hop and Latin records that nobody else has. The Beastie Boys immortalised the shop in their song 'Professor Booty'. *687 Haight St. | Muni 7 – Haight, 71 – Haight-Noriega*

GUITAR CENTER (124 B4) (*M N5*)

A huge shop with almost all the electric or electronically-amplified guitars available. *1645 Van Ness Ave. | Muni 1 – California*

GAMES & TOYS

GAMESCAPE (129 E1) (*M L8*)

So many (board) games that it is almost criminal. Daily session with table-top titles such as *Warhammer* and *Magic: The Gathering*. *333 Divisadero | Muni 21 – Hayes*

JEFFREY'S TOYS (125 D4) (*M Q5*)

The big chains have disappeared but this privately-run shop has managed to stay alive: Board games, hand puppets, construction kits and also comics (!) – a great selection. *685 Market St. | Muni F – Market*

WINE

NAPA VALLEY WINERY EXCHANGE (124 C4) (*M O5*)

If you don't get to Napa Valley itself, this is the best place to stock up on Californian wines and champagne; there are also many rare and unusual vintages. Your purchases will be put into airline packs for transport. *415 Taylor St. | Muni 38 – Geary*

ENTERTAINMENT

WHERE TO START?
You will look in vain for a beach at **North Beach (122 C3)** *(∅ 0–P 2–3)* but there is effervescent nightlife here between Downtown and China-town. Live music booms out of the bars, the owners of Italian restau-rants sing the praises of their kitchen and art lovers wander through gal-leries with a glass of wine in their hand. The Muni bus (30 – Stockton) will take you to where it is all hap-pening as it is virtually impossible to find a parking space.

If there are two cities in North America where nightlife is a *raison d'être*, they would have to be New York and San Francisco. The city on the Bay is much smaller than *The Big Apple* but it has almost as varied a programme to offer. Discos and nightclubs – it is all here and it is all world class.

The free papers *San Francisco Weekly* and *San Francisco Bay Guardian*, which are available in cafés and from newspaper machines, provide an overview of current events and keep you informed; they are also available online under *www.sfgate. com* and *www.sfstation.com*. Many bars, clubs and restaurants pay attention to

Photo: Cinema happening in the Castro Theatre

Hot clubs and cool bars – San Francisco offers something for all tastes

people being well-dressed – make sure you have a good shirt and possibly a jacket and dark shoes in your suitcase.

BARS & LOUNGES

ABSINTHE (124 B6) (*∅ N7*)
Orchestra musicians, concert visitors and bon vivants enjoy Carlos Yturria's fine cooking and absinthe cocktails –

the green liqueur is now legal again in the USA. *Closed Mon | 398 Hayes | Muni 21 – Fulton*

ALEMBIC (128 C2) (*∅ J8*)
This bar has more cocktails and varieties of whisky than you could get through in an evening. But, you should at least try a *Gilded Lily. Daily | 1725 Haight St. | Muni 75 – Haight/Noriega*

Vesuvio Café: the café bar is just as famous as the City Lights Bookstore opposite

BEACH CHALET & PARK CHALET ●
(126 A2) (*∅ A8*)

Have you had enough of the stiff breeze at Ocean Beach? Then it's time for happy hour and live music at the Beach Chalet or a drink on one of the sheltered deckchairs at the Park Chalet on the western edge of Golden Gate Park. *Daily | 1000 Great Highway | Muni 5 – Fulton*

INSIDER TIP BIG 4 RESTAURANT
(124 C4) (*∅ O5*)

Once you pass through the dark wooden swinging doors you will feel like you have travelled 100 years back in time: sophisticated music, attentive barkeepers and a 'No Cell Phones!' sign – wonderful! *Daily | 1075 California St. | Muni/Cable Car C – California*

GORDON BIERSCH (125 E4) (*∅ R5*)

People who grouse about American beer usually only know Budweiser and Miller. In most large cities you can now find local breweries like Gordon Biersch that serve different types of beer in different seasons. Cheers! *Daily | 2 Harrison St. | Muni N – Judah*

HOTEL UTAH SALOON (125 D5) (*∅ Q7*)

'The Utah' – as the locals call it – is in the SoMa multimedia district. But, not only 'dotcomers' relax here over beer and cocktails and listen to live music played by local bands – usually good rock. *Daily | 500 4th St. | Muni 30 – Stockton*

MEDJOOL (130 B4) (*∅ N10*)

It is a good idea to have something to eat from Medjool's outstanding Mediterranean menu before you drink one of the potent Mojitos in the lounge or on the roof terrace or go down to the basement to dance. *Daily | 2522 Mission St. | Muni 14 – Mission*

ORBIT ROOM (124 B6) (*∅ M8*)

Marble tables, scooters and a window for seeing and being seen – the epitome of the California feeling. *Daily | 1900 Market St. | Muni F – Market*

ROGUE ALES PUBLIC HOUSE
(124 C2) (*∅ P3*)

Hungry and thirsty from trekking around the city? In this pub, 40 draught beers, as well as many bottled varieties, burgers, salads and sandwiches await tourists and locals alike. *Daily | 673 Union St. | Muni 30 – Stockton*

SPECS (124 C3) (* crys P3*)
Insider's tip at North Beach: not only regulars drop by for a strong drink surrounded by maritime mementos. *Daily | 12 William Saroyan Place | Muni 30 – Stockton*

TOMMY'S MEXICAN RESTAURANT ★
(121 D5) (*crys E6*)
The Austrian bar-culture magazine 'Mixology' praises Tommy's as the world's best tequila bar. There is also outstanding Mexican food – it can be well worth making a trip to the west of town. *Closed Tue | 5929 Geary Blvd. | Muni 38 – Geary*

TOP OF THE MARK ⚜
(124 C4) (*crys P4*)
This nostalgic lounge with panoramic windows on all sides not only appeals to locals in the prime of life. *Daily | 1 Nob Hill | Cable Car C – California*

VESUVIO CAFÉ (124 C3) (*crys P4*)
In this legendary café-bar, famous for its authentic 1950s atmosphere, you will be reminded of Jack Kerouac and the beatniks and also see exhibitions of nude photography and works by local artists. *Daily | 255 Columbus Ave. | Muni 12 – Folsom*

INSIDER TIP ▶ WAYFARE TAVERN
(125 D3) (*crys Q4*)
Adam Richey is one of the best barkeepers in town. You simply must try his hot buttered rum at Christmas time. *Daily | 558 Sacramento St. | Muni 1 – California*

COMEDY CLUBS

BEACH BLANKET BABYLON ★
(124 C2) (*crys P3*)
It is always full here – the oddball musical revue has been running since 1974. The accent is on slapstick, the comedians wear enormous wigs and crazy costumes. Book online! *Wed–Sun | $25–130 | 68 Green St. | tel. 4 21 42 22 | www.beachblanketbabylon.com | Muni 30 – Stockton*

COBB'S COMEDY CLUB (124 B1) (*crys O3*)
Solo comedians have to show how good they really are here in North Beach – both local and nationally-known artists perform at Cobb's. *Thu–Sun | $20–30 plus two drinks | 915 Columbus Ave. | tel. 9 28 43 40 | www.cobbscomedy.com | Muni 30 – Stockton*

MARCO POLO HIGHLIGHTS

REDWOOD ROOM (124 C4) (*ⵘ O5*)
If you manage to get past the very selective bouncer, you might find yourself in the company of the singer and guitarist of Coldplay. Breathtaking ambience, beautiful waitresses, delicious martinis. *Daily | 495 Geary St. | Muni 38 – Geary*

DISCOS & NIGHTCLUBS

1015 FOLSOM (125 D5) (*ⵘ P7*)
The absolute dance factory for the young and chic crowd. Three floors with DJ, disco and acid jazz. Sometimes more yuppie, at other times more hip-hop. *Closed Sun–Wed | 1015 Folsom St. | tel. 4 31 74 44 | www.1015.com | Muni 12 – Folsom*

BIMBO'S 365 CLUB (124 C2) (*ⵘ O2*)
Bimbo's has been a real heavyweight in the club scene since 1931. Funk, jazz and electronica: the best musicians from the Bay area perform here. You should book in advance! *Various times and prices | 1025 Columbus Ave. | tel. 4 74 03 65 | www.bimbos365club | Muni 30 – Stockton*

BOOM BOOM ROOM (123 E5) (*ⵘ M6*)
The blues legend John Lee Hooker fulfilled a dream when he was more than 80 years old and opened his own club that – long after his death – is still hot. There is live music every day – a must, not only for blues fans. *Closed Mon | 1601 Fillmore St. | tel. 6 73 80 00 | www.boomboomblues.com | Muni 38 – Geary*

CAFÉ DU NORD ★ (129 E2) (*ⵘ M9*)
During the prohibition period, this nightclub that was opened in 1907 sold alcohol illegally. Standing at the 42-foot-long bar, you will have a feeling of how it was then. Alternative, folk and rock music. *Daily | small admission fee | 2170 Market St. | tel. 8 61 50 16 | www.cafedunord.com | Muni F – Market*

CIGAR BAR & GRILL (125 D3) (*ⵘ P4*)
This is a place to really let you hair down with a dance floor directly in front of alternating Latin bands, billiards under the stars – and smoking is expressly permitted. *Closed Sun | 850 Montgomery St. | Muni 12 – Folsom/Pacific*

DNA LOUNGE (130 C1) (*ⵘ O8*)
The former Netscape programmer Jamie Zawinski is now the boss of this nightclub. Webcams and blogs remind one of his roots. Mexican food, flamboyant, chic

RELAX & ENJOY

Are you tired from all of the dashing about? Don't worry; there are plenty of places waiting to get you back on your feet. The highly-qualified experts at ● *True Massage and Wellness* **(124 C4)** (*ⵘ P5*) *(daily | 760 Market St. | tel. 6 77 94 61)* are looking forward to going to work on your weary muscles and refreshing your body and spirit while the ● *Earth & Sky Oasis* **(124 C4)** (*ⵘ P5*) *(closed Mon | 391 Sutter St. | tel. 9 89 00 14)* also offers acupuncture treatment, as well as pedicures and manicures. And, the ☆ *Nob Hill Spa* in the Huntington Hotel **(124 C4)** (*ⵘ P5*) *(1075 California St. | tel. 474 54 00 | www.huntingtonhotel.com)* scores with a pool and fairy-tale view form the roof terrace while you are wrapped up in your bathrobe.

The bar and dance floor at Mr. Smith's: always full, always fun

public; and the most outlandish characters in town come to the theme evenings. *Closed Tue/Wed | 375 11th St. | tel. 626 1409 | www.dnalounge.com | Muni 9 – San Bruno*

HENRY DENTON'S STARLIGHT ROOM
⤒ *(124 C4) (𝖒 P5)*

An illustrious group of locals and tourists of all ages get together here on the 21st floor of the Sir Francis Drake Hotel to enjoy the view, music and drinks. Sunday brunch with a drag show. *Closed Mon | 450 Powell St. | Muni 2 – Clement, F – Market*

THE INDEPENDENT *(123 E6) (𝖒 L7)*

A musical institution for more than 30 years. Local and international up-and-coming artists, as well as top acts such as DJ Shadow, Erasure and Henry Rollins, perform here. Good sound system, accomplished barkeepers and tolerant bouncers. *Various times and prices | 628 Divisadero St. | tel. 711421 | www.theindependentsf. com | Muni 21 – Hayes*

MR. SMITH'S ⭐ *(124 C5) (𝖒 O7)*

With this club, the managers Kevin and Max opened a real gem: laid-back bar, cool lounge and dancing on three floors – easygoing bouncers, adept barkeepers and good DJs. *Closed Sun/Mon | 34 7th St. | Muni F – Market*

INSIDER TIP ▶ RED DEVIL LOUNGE
(124 B3) (𝖒 N4)

This small, carefree neighbourhood club can boast stars such as *The Commitments* and *ABC*. Newcomers are also given a chance. *Various times and prices | 1695 Polk St. | www.reddevillounge.com | Muni 19 – Polk*

YOSHI'S JAZZ CLUB ⭐
(123 E5) (𝖒 M6)

San Francisco's top jazz address has been branching out into other genres since 2009. Stars such as Marcus Miller, Leo Kottke and Abdullah Ibrahim alternate with up-and-coming musicians. The Japanese cuisine is also first-rate. *Daily |*

CINEMAS

1330 Fillmore St. | www.yoshis.com | Muni 22 – Fillmore

CINEMAS

BALBOA THEATRE (126 C1) *(⋒ C7)*
Built in 1926, this cinema has doggedly held its own against all the Multiplex palaces. Classics and new films, low admission fees – free on your birthday! *Daily | 3630 Balboa St. | www.balboamovies. com | Muni 31 – Balboa*

CASTRO THEATRE ★
(129 E3) *(⋒ L9)*
This magnificent cinematic palace with 1500 seats, a tent-like dome and a gigantic trompe-l'œil painting mainly shows film classics. Silent films are often accom-

LOW BUDGET

▶ The *Anchor Steam Brewery* **(131 D2)** *(⋒ Q9)* has produced steam beer since 1896 and is the only one doing so in the United States. You can try out the various types of beer on a two-hour, free tour of the brewery. It is necessary to book far in advance! *1705 Mariposa St. | tel. 8 63 83 50 | Muni 19 – Polk*

▶ ● *Opera/Shakespeare in the Park*: there are many free opera and theatre performances in the city's parks between May and September. Have a look at the up-to-date programme under: *www.sfopera.com, www. sfshakes.org*. Half-price tickets for performances on the same day are available at the ticket booth on *Union Square* **(124 C5)** *(⋒ P5)*. *Muni Cable Car PH – Powell & Hyde*

panied by a cinema orchestra or live organ music. *429 Castro St. | tel. 6 21 61 20 | www.castrotheatre.com |Muni F – Market*

INSIDER TIP **LUMIERE THEATRE**
(124 B4) *(⋒ N5)*
Small, high-class repertory cinema that shows films you won't see anywhere else – often in the original language with subtitles. *1572 California St. | tel. 2 67 48 93 | Cable Car C – California*

CLASSICAL MUSIC & BALLET

POCKET OPERA
From March to July, this miniature opera gives very informal performances, without extravagant costumes, at a number of locations such as the *Waterfront Theater*, on Ghirardelli Square or in the *Florence Gould Theater. 469 Bryant St. | tel. 9 72 89 30 | www.pocketopera.org*

SAN FRANCISCO OPERA COMPANY
(124 B5) *(⋒ N7)*
The short season begins in September and only lasts 14 weeks meaning that the house, with its world-class performances, is usually sold out. The ballet season follows from January to May and it is also advisable to book as early as possible for these events. *War Memorial Opera House | 301 Van Ness Ave. | tel. 8 61 40 08 | www.sfopera.com | Muni 21 – Hayes*

SAN FRANCISCO SYMPHONY ●
(124 B6) *(⋒ N7)*
The award-winning symphony orchestra celebrated its 100th anniversary in 2011. Michael Tilson Thomas (Los Angeles), its chief conductor since 1995, is a specialist for works by American composers, as well as Mahler and Stravinsky. The inexpensive public rehearsals in the morning and afternoon concerts are especially popular. *Davies Symphony Hall | 210 Van Ness Ave. |*

Internationally famous singers and ballet dancers appear in the sumptuous San Francisco Opera

tel. 8 64 60 00 | www.sfsymphony.org | Muni 21 – Hayes

MUSICALS

CURRAN THEATRE
(124 C4) (𝄞 O5)
Comedies and musicals from Broadway, and sometimes even Shakespeare. *445 Geary St. | tel. 5 512 00 | Muni 38 – Geary*

GOLDEN GATE THEATRE
(124 C5) (𝄞 P6)
Famous musicals (Phantom of the Opera, Chicago, Hair) performed in a magnificent building opened in 1922. *1 Taylor St. | tel. 5 512 00 | shnsf.com/theatres/golden gate | Muni F – Market*

ORPHEUM THEATRE (124 C5) (𝄞 O7)
Old favourites, as well as new Broadway musicals to delight all the family. *1192 Market St. | tel. 5 517 70 | www.orpheum theatretickets.com | Muni F – Market*

THEATRES

AMERICAN CONSERVATORY THEATER
(124 C4) (𝄞 P5)
The address for lovers of traditional theatre. The most dynamic group in San Francisco – comparable to the British National Theatre – performs at various locations in the city throughout the year. *415 Geary St. | tel. 7 49 22 28 | www.act-sf.org | Muni 38 – Geary*

EUREKA THEATER COMPANY
(125 D3) (𝄞 Q4)
Modern productions of mainly social and political plays performed in an art-déco theatre. *215 Jackson St. | tel. 7 88 74 69 | www.eurekatheater.org | Muni 1 – California*

MAGIC THEATRE (124 A1) (𝄞 M2)
This is the place to see old and new plays by American authors such as Sam Shepard and Nilo Cruz. *Building D | Fort Mason | tel. 4 41 88 22 | Muni 30 – Stockton*

WHERE TO STAY

After New York, San Francisco is the most expensive city in the USA – it is not at all difficult to pay $1800 a month for a simple, two-room flat. Hotel prices from 200 to 300 dollars a night are no exception.

Along with the large, often expensive, hotels, there is a new trend towards boutique hotels: old buildings have been bought, renovated and now offer reasonably-priced rooms.

Bed & breakfast in a Victorian house can be less expensive but this is not always the case – it is always a good idea to compare prices, just as it is in the hotels that have now been opened in the old mansions, the erstwhile palatial residences of wealthy San Franciscans. One way for families and groups to save money is to look for multi-bed rooms in motels and hostels. But don't forget, 15.5% guest tax is always added to the price of each room.

The high season is from the beginning of May to the end of September but it is worth visiting San Francisco at any time – there is always something happening! In addition, many hotels are happy to have guests in the off-season and offer considerably reduced prices. The room rates in some hotels in the moderate price category almost fall to the level of the budget category.

Photo: Lobby of the Fairmont Hotel

California dreamin' – a city with palatial hotels as well as more intimate guesthouses in fine locations

You can also make big savings if you book online: many hotels promote internet prices that cannot be beaten anywhere. Your credit card will be charged when you make the booking or when you check in; the same applies to telephone reservations. You will find interesting offers on many websites including *www.expedia.com, www.hotels.com, www.kayak.com, www. priceline.com* and *www.hotwire.com*.

HOTELS: EXPENSIVE

CLIFT HOTEL (124 C4) (*O5*)

This 'wonderland for the jet set' was built in 1913. Today, it is in the hands of the ultra-chic *Morgans Hotel Group* (as well as the Mondrian, Los Angeles and Hudson, New York) and its main designer Philippe Starck. Modern luxury with paintings by Dalí and Magritte in the lobby. Clift guests

Design mixture between avant-garde and eccentric, but – in any case – original: Hotel Triton

have no problems getting into the *Redwood Room* (see: Entertainment, p. 84). *363 rooms | 495 Geary St. | tel. 7 75 47 00 | www.clifthotel.com | Muni 38 – Geary*

FAIRMONT HOTEL ★ ☙
(124 C3) (*ɯ P4*)
This palace of marble on Nob Hill is probably the most famous hotel in San Francisco. In the cellar: the *Tonga Room*, a tiki bar with tropical storms and a live band playing on a boat. Many of the luxurious rooms have magnificent views of the Downtown district, Alcatraz and the Bay area. *591 rooms | 950 Mason St. | tel. 7 72 50 00 | www.fairmont.com/sanfrancisco | Cable Car C – California*

HOTEL TRITON (124 C4) (*ɯ P5*)
This extravagant hotel on Union Square is one of the group of boutique hotels that are often eccentrically furnished. Nine local artists decorated the rooms and each one is unique including the hand-painted 'Diamond Room' and 'Tomato Soup Room'. Before you make your final choice, you should look at some of the most interesting rooms on the hotel's website. *140 rooms | 342 Grant Ave. | tel. 3 94 05 00 | www.hoteltriton.com | Muni 2 – Clement*

MANDARIN ORIENTAL ☙
(125 D3) (*ɯ Q4*)
The view from the windows of the hotel on the top floors of the California Center is absolutely exquisite. That is why they are all equipped with binoculars. Service is given high priority in the award-winning hotel. *154 rooms | 222 Sansome St. | tel. 2 76 98 88 | www.mandarinoriental. com / Cable Car – C*

PALACE HOTEL
(125 D4) (ɰ Q5)

The hotel hall, which has been preserved almost entirely as it was in 1875, is absolutely unique and the interior garden also breathes the grandezza of the founding years. Spacious rooms. Online bookings are often less expensive. *522 rooms and suites | 2 New Montgomery St. | tel. 512 1111 | www.sfpalace.com | Muni F – Market*

W SAN FRANCISCO ★ ☺
(125 D4) (ɰ Q6)

The management of the modern 'W' feel that is most important that all their guests have a good time here: locals and visitors get together for a drink in the *XYZ Bar*. The building has been certified by the U.S. Green Building Council since 2010. *423 rooms | 181 3rd St. | tel. 7775300 | www.whotels.com | Muni 30 – Stockton*

HOTELS: MODERATE

HOTEL ADAGIO
(124 C4) (ɰ O5)

Old meets new: the Spanish-colonial-revival style building is the home of a smart boutique hotel. The 80 rooms have a fine view and the Adagio Bar on the ground floor will tempt you to have a drink or two. *171 rooms | 550 Geary St. | tel. 775 9388 | www.jdvhotels.com/hotels/adagio | Muni 38 - Geary*

INSIDER TIP ▶ BOHÈME
(125 D2) (ɰ P3)

The name says it all: the decoration makes a conscious reference to the culture and taste of the beat generation of the 1950s. And this, in North Beach where the bohemians used to live. The rooms are tiny but the lavender or lime-green paint will make up for it. *15 rooms | 444 Columbus St. | tel. 4339111 | www.hotel boheme.com | Muni 30 – Stockton*

THE CHATEAU TIVOLI ★
(123 E6) (ɰ L6)

If you want to live in style in one of the Victorian houses known as the *Painted Ladies*, you should book a room in the Chateau Tivoli. The cosy bed & breakfast near Alamo Square was built in 1892 and will charm you with its breathtaking, period furnishings. There are some less expensive rooms if you are prepared to share a

---

MARCO POLO HIGHLIGHTS

★ **Fairmont Hotel**
Magnificent lobby and fantastic view of the city → p. 90

★ **W San Francisco**
Chic hotel, chic guests – and a chic DJ takes care of the music → p. 91

★ **The Chateau Tivoli**
Antiques and four-poster beds in a former private residence → p. 91

★ **Ritz Carlton**
The classic luxury hotel → p. 92

★ **Golden Gate**
The city house Europeans are particularly fond of → p. 92

★ **Petite Auberge**
Charming villa with a Victorian exterior and Provençal interior → p. 94

★ **Phoenix Hotel**
This is where many a Hollywood star stays in San Francisco → p. 94

★ **Queen Anne Hotel**
Victorian, practical, good – located on the edge of Pacific Heights → p. 95

LUXURY HOTELS

Campton Place (122 C4) (*P5*)
A completely renovated hotel with marble bathrooms, concealed televisions and exceptional service in a building from the turn of the century. From $300. *101 rooms, 9 suites | 340 Stockton St. | www.camptonplace.com | Muni 30 – Stockton, 45 – Union/Stockton*

Four Seasons ♨ (123 D4) (*P5*)
This hotel at the Moscone Conference Center is modern but extremely comfortable. All the rooms are spacious and have a fine panoramic view of San Francisco Bay. The guests can also use the 97,000 ft² fitness centre in the basement – complete with training courses and pool. From $495. *231 rooms, 46 suites | 757 Market St. | tel. 6 33 30 00 | www.fourseasons.com | Muni F – market*

Huntington (122 C4) (*O5*)
One of the most elegant hotels in America; Gregory Peck even stayed here. Discreet, full of antiques and with an outstanding restaurant. From $335. *96 rooms, 40 suites | 1075 California St. | tel. 4 74 54 00 | www.huntingtonhotel.com | Cable Car C – California*

Hyatt Regency (123 D3) (*Q4*)
The peak of luxury around a 17-floor atrium open at the top; this is especially the case on the club floors with their private bars and concierges. From $230. *757 rooms, 45 suites | 5 Embarcadero Center | tel. 7 88 12 34 | www.sanfrancisco regency.hyatt.com | Muni 1 – California, Cable Car C – California*

Mark Hopkins ♨ (122 C4) (*P4*)
Located high up on Nob Hill with a magnificent view that is especially impressive from the suites. There, you can admire the surroundings from the comfort of your whirlpool. Top-of-the-Mark Lounge on the 19th floor. From $180. *382 rooms, 33 suites | 1 Nob Hill | tel. 3 92 34 34 | www.intercontinental.com | Cable Car C – California*

Ritz Carlton ★ ♨ (122 C3) (*P4*)
This has been *the* luxury hotel on Nob Hill since it opened in 1991. It has everything you could want: two excellent restaurants, a fitness centre and pool, as well as a business centre and a club floor with concierge. From $460. *227 rooms, 60 suites | 600 Stockton St. | tel. 2 96 74 65 | www.ritzcarlton.com/hotels/san_ francisco | Cable Car C – California*

bathroom with other guests. *22 rooms | 1057 Steiner St. | tel. 7 76 54 62 | www. chateautivoli.com | Muni 5 – Fulton*

DONATELLO HOTEL
(124 C4) (*P5*)
This is as central as it gets: the Donatello is located only one block from Union Square. Spacious, modern rooms, a whirl-

pool and sauna will help you recover from all the stress of shopping. *94 rooms | 501 Post St. | tel. 441-7100 | www.thedonatellosf. com | Muni 2 – Clement*

GOLDEN GATE ★ (124 C4) (*P5*)
Bed & breakfast in a cosy turn-of-the-century house with a narrow façade, bay windows and an old-fashioned wire-cage

lift – and around half of the guests come from Europe. Not all of the 25 rooms have an en suite bathroom but the owners, with their cats and dogs, are extremely friendly and helpful. *775 Bush St. | tel. 3 92 37 02, 80 08 35 11 18 | www.goldengatehotel. com | Muni 2 – Clement*

INSIDER TIP **INN ON CASTRO**
(129 E2) (*∅ L9*)

This inn was opened in one of the more charming *Edwardian houses* almost in the centre of the Castro district. The rooms – all but one have en suite bathrooms – are modern and cheerful. Most open onto a

The impressive 17-story atrium lobby of the Hyatt Regency palace of luxury

THE GOOD HOTEL ☺
(124 C5) (*∅ P7*)

This hotel in the slightly suspect SoMa district gives high priority to recycling, reuses waste water and even has four free bicycles for its early-rising guests to use. *117 rooms | 112 7th St. | tel. 6 21 70 01 | www. thegoodhotel.com | Muni F – Market*

HANDLERY UNION SQUARE
(124 C4) (*∅ P5*)

A classical, charmingly renovated, inner-city hotel; club guests who pay a little more also have access to a sauna and swimming pool. *377 rooms | 351 Geary St. | tel. 7 81 78 00 | tel. 80 08 43 43 43 | www. handlery.com | Muni 38 – Geary*

small patio; the suite has a small garden. *7 rooms, 1 suite | 321 Castro St. | tel. 8 61 03 21 | www.innoncastro.com | Muni F – Market*

KING GEORGE (124 C4) (*∅ P5*)

Elegant lobby, all of the rooms decorated in soft pastel tones, a good Japanese restaurant and a location close to Union Square – what more could you ask for? *153 rooms | 334 Mason St. | tel. 7 81 50 50 | www.kinggeorge.com | Muni 38 – Geary*

MARINA MOTEL (123 D2) (*∅ K3*)

The rooms in this motel need to be spruced up a little and it is a bit loud but there are also rooms on the courtyard and many

The Phoenix Phoenix Hotel is popular with artists and musicians

restaurants and bars in the neighbourhood. Some of the rooms even have a kitchenette – ask for one. One important plus point: parking is free! *36 rooms | 2576 Lombard St. | tel. 9 21 94 06 | www.marinamotel.com | Muni 30 – Stockton*

INSIDER TIP THE MOSSER HOTEL ☺ (124 C4) (*ᗰ P6*)

In 1981, Charles W. Mosser bought a hotel, renovated it and installed a sound studio where he could record some of the 5000 songs he had written himself. You can book the studio as a package with your room and record your own CD. Part of the hotel's profits goes to charity organisations including those with the goal of preserving rainforests. *166 rooms | 54 Fourth St. | tel. 9 86 44 00 | www.themosser.com | Muni F – Market*

NOB HILL HOTEL (124 B4) (*ᗰ O5*)

You will feel like you have travelled back to San Francisco in the early 20th century in this stylishly decorated hotel with its stucco ceilings and billowing curtains; breakfast, newspapers and afternoon wine tastings are all included. *53 rooms |* *835 Hyde St. | tel. 8 85 29 87 | www.nobhillhotel.com | Muni 27 Bryant*

PARK FIFTY FIVE ☆ (124 C5) (*ᗰ P6*)

Airline crews from all over the world like to unwind in this multi-storey business hotel with spectacular views that was revamped to its present cool, hip style in 2009. *1010 rooms, 18 suites | 55 Cyril Magnin St. | tel. 3 92 80 00 | www.parc55hotel.com | Muni F – Market*

PETITE AUBERGE ★ (124 C4) (*ᗰ O5*)

Bed & breakfast with the feeling of a French manor house. The teddy bears scattered around are a bit kitschy but there is a fabulous breakfast and the hors d'œuvres and sherry served in the lounge in the afternoon are really delicious. *26 rooms | 863 Bush St. | tel. 9 28 60 00 | tel. 80 03 65 30 04 | www.jdvhotels.com/petite_auberge | Muni 2 - Clement*

PHOENIX HOTEL ★ (124 B5) (*ᗰ N–O6*)

This hotel is not in one of San Francisco's most salubrious neighbourhoods but the notorious Tenderloin district. However, this does not appear to bother the film makers, rock musicians, writers and other artists who like to stay at the Phoenix. The rooms are enormous and decorated with bamboo furniture, and there is also a heated swimming pool in the courtyard. *44 rooms | 601 Eddy St. | tel. 7 76 13 80 | www.jdvhospitality.com | Muni 31 – Balboa*

QUEEN ANNE HOTEL ⭐
(123 E4) (*M5*)

When the hotel was built more than 100 years ago it was located outside the city. Now it is inside – in the Western Addition. This is not considered a really top-notch district but is obviously not so bad that a luxuriously-decorated Victorian bed & breakfast could not be established here. The rooms are decorated with English antiques and have hand-made wooden floors. *49 rooms and suites | 1590 Sutter St. | tel. 4 41 28 28 | www.queenanne.com | Muni 2 – Clement*

STANYAN PARK HOTEL
(128 C2) (*J8*)

This especially charming three-storey building built in 1905 is another Victorian gem. The six, reasonably priced, suites can accommodate up to six people making them ideal for families and groups of friends. *Directly at Golden Gate Park. 36 rooms, 6 suites | 750 Stanyan St. | tel. 7 51 10 00 | www.stanyanpark.com | Muni 1 – Haight/Noriega*

HOTELS: BUDGET

ADELAIDE HOSTEL (124 C4) (*O5*)

The Adelaide Hostel offers six small but clean rooms with private bathrooms and also uses the facilities of the neighbouring Hotel Dakota. This is accompanied by breakfast, internet access, friendly service and lounges. *86 rooms | 5 Isadora Duncan Lane |*

tel. 3 59 19 15 | www.adelaidehostel.com | Muni 38 – Geary

INSIDER TIP ▶ **HOTEL DES ARTS**
(124 C4) (*P5*)

Most of the rooms have been individually decorated by up-and-coming artists – they are so cool that you will hardly want to leave them. That would be a pity because Chinatown and Downtown are both only one block away. Breakfast and internet are included; fabulous online specials. *43 rooms | 447 Bust St. | tel. 9 56 32 32 |*

LOW BUDGET

Even in the homeland of capitalism, there are 😊 cooperative hotels that have the aim of making a contribution to intercultural understanding and to dealing responsibly with the environment. The rather simple accommodation is more than compensated for by the low prices – and, in the case of the Fisherman's Wharf Hostel, by a unique location in Fort Mason right on the waterfront. The three hostels *(www.sfhostels.com)*:

▶ City Center **(124 B5)** (*O6*): *dormitories from $25, private rooms from $79 | 685 Ellis St. | tel. 4 74 57 21 | Muni 38 – Geary*

▶ Downtown **(124 C4)** (*P5*): *dormitories from $27, private rooms from $69 | 312 Mason St. | tel. 7 88 56 04 | Muni 38 – Geary*

▶ Fisherman's Wharf ⚓ **(123 E1)** (*M2*): *dormitories from $26, private rooms from $65 | Fort Mason, Building 240 | tel. 7 71 72 77 | Muni 30 – Stockton*

www.sfhoteldesarts.com | Muni 2 – Clement

GRANT PLAZA HOTEL (124 C3) (*P5*)
If you are travelling without much money in your wallet and still want to stay in a centrally located hotel, the Grant Plaza in the heart of Chinatown could be just what you're looking for. The rooms are tiny but spotlessly clean. To make up for this, you are just a short walk away from Union Square and North Beach. *72 rooms | 465 Grant Ave. | tel. 4 34 38 83 | www.grantplaza.com | Muni 30 – Stockton*

HAYES VALLEY INN (124 A6) (*N7*)
This easy-going, family-owned hotel claims to be a 'home away from home'. Bright, cheerful rooms, friendly staff, breakfast included and really pleasing prices. Restaurants and shops just around the corner. *28 rooms | 417 Gough St. | tel. 4 31 91 31 | www.hayesvalleyinn.com | Muni 21 – Hayes*

INSIDER TIP LUZ HOTEL (124 B4) (*O5*)
The motto of this really charming hotel is 'Come as guests, leave as family'. Very simple but clean rooms – most of them share a bathroom. Unbelievably inexpensive: from $50 per night or $350 per week including taxes and internet access.

Friendly, helpful staff. *22 rooms | 725 Geary St. | tel. 9 28 19 17 | www.luzhotelsf.com | Muni 38 – Geary*

HOTEL MAYFLOWER (124 C4) (*O5*)
Things that were a bit of a sensation in 1929 are still not standard today: most of the large rooms also have a basin, refrigerator and even a microwave. The theatre district, Chinatown and Union Square are only a few minutes' walk away. And, breakfast and internet are also included in the price. *102 rooms | 975 Bush St. | tel. 6 73 70 10 | www.sfmayflowerhotel.com | Muni 27 – Bryant*

METRO HOTEL (123 E6) (*L8*)
A genuine gem on the border of Lower and Upper Haight – in five minutes, you can be in the centre of Haight-Ashbury or the more orthodox territory of Lower Haight. It is best to book online because the hotel is very popular in spite of its small rooms. *23 rooms | 319 Divisadero St. | tel. 8 61 53 64 | www.metrohotelsf.com | Muni 71 – Haight/Noriega*

INSIDER TIP HOTEL METROPOLIS (124 C5) (*P6*)
As soon as you walk into the Metropolis, you leave the hectic rush of the big city behind you. A library on the first floor and

LIVE LIKE THE LOCALS

Be a San Franciscan. If you don't want to stay in a hotel and are brave enough, you can live as a subtenant for a couple of weeks. If you look under *sublet* on *sfbay.craigslist.org*, you will find a list of flats that can be rented for a short period. If you only want to stay for a few nights, more than 3000 San

Franciscans offer everything from a sofa bed to your own room on *www.couchsurfing.com*; *www.hospitalityclub.org* and *www.globalfreeloaders* provide a similar service. Who knows, you might be lucky and be able to consider yourself a real San Franciscan for a while.

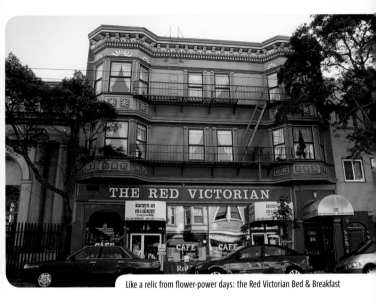

Like a relic from flower-power days: the Red Victorian Bed & Breakfast

a Zen rest room invite you to relax and the colours of the rooms reflect the elements of earth, air, fire and water. The *Farmer Brown Restaurant* with wonderful comfort food is attached to the hotel; it serves beer in old preserving jars and also has a Sunday brunch with live music. Try the *fried chicken with macaroni and cheese*. *105 rooms | 25 Mason St. | tel. 7 75 46 00 | www.hotelmetropolis.com | Muni F – Market*

THE RED VICTORIAN, BED, BREAKFAST & ART (128 C2) (*J8*)

This is the place where a hippie's dreams can come true. Nostalgia in its purest form is the order of the day in this B&B which its guests lovingly call the Red Vic, on Haight Street. Each of the rooms is decorated in keeping with a different motto: *Summer of Love, Earth Charter Room, Japanese Tea Garden* or *Sami's Poster Room*. There is even a meditation room. The main target group is young travellers who are not bothered by the fact that they will have to clamber over all of the homeless people on Haight Street in the morning. But, it is still a good idea to book early! *18 rooms | 1665 Haight St. | tel. 8 64 19 78 | www.redvic. com | Muni 71 – Haight*

INSIDER**TIP** ▶ **SAN REMO**
(124 B–C2) (*O2*)
This hotel is in a peaceful section of North Beach but still within walking distance of Fisherman's Wharf. There is hardly a better location in San Francisco. The rooms are decorated in an American rural style: brass and steel beds, wooden and cane furniture, and ceiling fans. The bathrooms – none are en suite – still have free-standing tubs where wild-west heroes would feel completely at home. The penthouse is especially lovely. *62 rooms | 2237 Mason St. / corner of Chestnut St. | tel. 7 76 86 88 | www.sanremohotel.com | Cable Car PM – Powell & Mason*

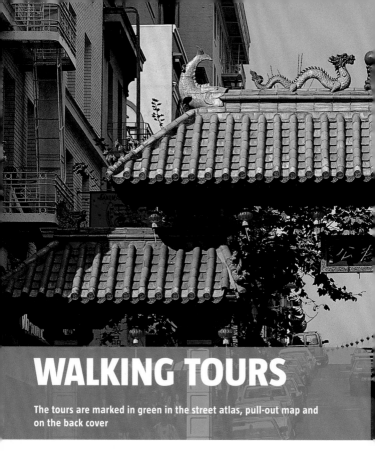

WALKING TOURS

The tours are marked in green in the street atlas, pull-out map and on the back cover

1 ALONG THE BAY –
BEAUTIFUL VIEWS AND
HARDLY ANY HILLS

If you've had enough of climbing up and down the hills of San Francisco, a long walk along the water is just what you need. You should count on the whole tour taking six to eight hours – unless you do it by bike.

The starting point is **Aquatic Park**. Alcatraz and the museum ships are on the right; your goal is on the left: the **Golden Gate Bridge → p. 29**. Stay next to the water and walk along McDowell Avenue, a former access road to **Fort Mason → p. 34**. You

pass a small park; stay on the right and walk up the hill to Marina Boulevard. On the left: the Safeway Supermarket *(open 24 hours a day | 15 Marina Blvd.)* immortalised in Armistead Maupin's 'Tales of the City' as a meeting place for singles. Why not buy a freshly-made sandwich to give you some energy?

Back on the other side of the street, walk past the marina towards the west. You will have a splendid view of Fort Mason from **Marina Green Drive** between the yacht and western harbours. Turn left onto Scott Street and then right onto Marina Boulevard where you will see the **Palace of Fine Arts → p. 36** on the right,

Photo: Gate to Chinatown

It takes more than culture and shopping to make people happy – enjoy a day on the Bay

but you are not going to visit it today. Road construction work made it necessary to transfer the **Crissy Field Center** *(daily Q 1199 East Beach)* to its present location here on the right. This is a good opportunity to have a coffee and get some information on the former Crissy Field military airfield. You can reach it by taking the diagonal footpath from Lyon Street towards **Golden Gate Promenade** → p. 30.

Proceeding further to the west, you will pass the Farralone Visitor Center, the Warming Hut and then finally reach **Fort Point** → p. 29.
Continue back towards the city along the path 500 yards to the east of Fort Point that winds its way up towards the south side of the Golden Gate Bridge. Depending on the time and weather, you should at least walk to the first pier of the bridge

How about a quick trip to Japan? The Japanese Tea garden in the middle of Golden Gate Park

and then catch bus 28 towards Fort Mason at the visitors' park; get off at the last stop and walk back to Aquatic Park.

If it is not too late, we recommended visiting the museum ships anchored at **Hyde Street Pier** → p. 48, the small Sailors' Church or the **Musée Mécanique** → p. 50 at Pier 45. Finish the tour with dinner at Fisherman's Grotto 9 *(daily | 2847 Taylor St. | tel. 6 73 70 25 | Moderate)* – the fish-dish of the day is usually very good. If you are still up to it, walk along Jefferson Street and The Embarcadero until you reach the **Ferry Building** → p. 56 to have one of the hot tea or coffee specialities served at **Peet's Coffee & Tea** *(daily)*.

2 49 MILES – THIS TIME BY CAR

This time you will really drive 78.5 km (49 mi) through all of San Francisco. You would have to be very fit otherwise to walk this in one go! That is why it is better to make this sight-seeing trip American style: in the comfort of your car. If you take your time and get out now and then to take your souvenir photos instead of just winding down the windows to shoot them, this tour will take around four hours.

The tour starts wherever your hotel is – probably in the city centre. If you are just making a stopover in San Francisco and are coming from the airport, take Highway 101 North to the 'Cesar Chavez' exit. You will soon see the small signs with a white seagull on a blue background and the inscription '49 Mile Scenic Drive'. It passes the **Embarcadero** with a view of the **Bay Bridge** → p. 54. From there, drive down central **Market Street** → p. 57, past the Visitor Information Center and **City Hall** → p. 54. Now it starts to get hilly; after the bend around the Japan Center you drive up elegant **Nob Hill** and from there into the heart of **Chinatown**. The route then takes you down Grant Avenue to the Italian **North Beach** district. You once again reach sea level at **Fisherman's Wharf** → p. 43.

Drive around **Fort Mason** → p. 34, past the marina to the **Exploratorium** → p. 104 with the **Palace of Fine Arts** → p. 36. This is a good place for culture aficionados to take a break and an even better one for those interested in the secrets of science. Drive through **Presidio** → p. 32 to **Fort Point** → p. 29. You will simply have to stop here; you are right under the **Golden Gate Bridge** → p. 29.

Continue driving through Presidio; this time, on the Pacific Ocean side where you will get your first glimpse of the wide open sea. Drive to the south past **Seal Rocks** and the ☼ **Cliff House** → p. 28 (a good place to have lunch) along the Great Highway with the raging ocean below you and seals and sea lions basking in the sun on the rocks.

Drive around Lake Merced. The parks it lies in are full of golf courses. The most interesting part of this tour starts north of Sunset Boulevard in **Golden Gate Park** → p. 40. There are many lovely spots to take a break and stretch your legs: at the **Japanese Tea Garden** → p. 41, the **De Young Museum** → p. 40, the **California Academy of Sciences** → p. 38, as well as at the **National Aids Memorial Grove**, a park established to commemorate all of the victims of the disease.

In a wide arch to the south, you approach ☼ **Twin Peaks** → p. 43. This is definitely one of the highlights for lovers of magnificent views. Driving down from the two hills, you will also see many other lovely panoramas of the city and Bay. Turn onto Dolores Street from 14th street and head south to the last stop at the **Mission Dolores** → p. 42. This Spanish mission church is the northernmost in a series

stretching from the Mexican border – each of them was one day's ride from the next. At the end of Dolores Street, which takes you through the Latino district, you will once again reach Cesar Chavez Street that soon crosses Highway 101. A better way to get back to town is by taking Highway 280 that leads to the **South Beach** area bordering on the **South of Market** district.

You should return your car here – or at least park it. It is much better to explore the centre on foot, by taxi or using public transport. If you want, you can let the day come to an end in SoMa. The **Lulu** Restaurant *(daily | 816 Folsom St/corner of 4th St. | Moderate)* with its American-Mediterranean atmosphere is the perfect place to wind down in.

③ THE NORTH-WEST – THE PACIFIC, WEALTH & HISTORY

The approx. 6 km (4 mi) walk along the Lands End Trail to the Golden Gate Bridge is not especially strenuous and a real pleasure at any time of the year. It will take 2–3 hours; make sure you are wearing sturdy shoes and have enough water with you.

It starts at the **Point Lobos** and **48th Avenue** junction (123 B5) *(₥ A6)*; the best way to get there is by taking the bus *(Muni 38 – Geary)*. Going towards the sea, you will reach a large car park on Point Lobos Avenue with a path at its northern end leading to the ruins of the **Sutro Baths**; an interesting detour. If your stomach starts to rumble, or if you want to have a sandwich to eat on the way, you can take care of things at the restaurant in the **Cliff House** → p. 28 adjacent to the Sutro Baths or at Louis'. Back to the car park: A hiking path begins at its northern end that leads in a bend to the **Lands End Trail** where, 120 years ago, people could take the train into or out of town for a fare of a mere 5 cents.

Legion of Honor: the appropriate setting for a temple to the arts

Don't take the turn to the right unless you want to climb up the steps to the **Palace of the Legion of Honor** → p. 31 and then down them again. The sign-posted path follows the water's edge to Mile Rock Beach on the left from where another path takes you to the **Eagle Point** lookout and the labyrinth. At low tide, you will be able to see many shipwrecks from the 1920s and '30s.

The **Lands End Trail** joins **El Camino Del Mar** that winds its way through San Francisco's wealthy **Sea Cliff** district with its exorbitantly priced villas. Keep going further to the north until the road meets Sea Cliff Avenue that soon bends to the right. Turn left onto 25th Avenue – a cul-de-sac, but on the left there is a path down to **Baker Beach** → p. 28 with spectacular views of the **Golden Gate Bridge** and **Marin Headlands**.

When you reach the **Battery Chamberlain**, one of a total of 17 cannon batteries installed at Fort Scott between 1891 and 1946, follow the beach path and find your way to Lincoln Boulevard that you walk along in a northerly direction until you come to another path to the beach after a zebra crossing. Going past the Battery Crosby, Marshall Beach, Battery Boutelle and Battery Cranston, you will ultimately reach the southern end of the **Golden Gate Bridge** → p. 29. Here, you can catch the Muni-Bus 28 that will take you back to **Fisherman's Wharf** → p. 43.

4 A STROLL THROUGH SAUSALITO AND TIBURON

You can reach Sausalito and Tiburon on the other side of the Bay by car or bicycle (first exit to the right after the Bridge) or by ferry if you prefer to arrive from the water. If you want to learn something about recent history on your way north, a detour to Angel Island can be recommended. The ferries of the *Blue & Gold Fleet (www. blueandgoldfleet.com)* offer return trips to Angel Island *($16)*, Sausalito *($21)* and Tiburon *($21)* departing from Pier 41.

The sun shines in these wealthier suburbs even when San Francisco is covered with fog. This has inspired the people living in the two small towns to become creative: you will find quite a few locally produced artefacts in galleries and boutiques.

Sausalito was founded in the middle of the 19th century and today its main street, the Bridgeway, with many boutiques, cafés and good restaurants such as INSIDER TIP **Le Garage** *(daily | 85 Liberty Ship Way, Suite 109 | tel. 3 32 56 25 | Moderate)* – a cult French bistro in a (you guessed it) former garage – attracts many visitors. You will see Sausalito's world-famous houseboat settlement, established by artists in the 1960s, on the right shortly before you reach the Bridgeway and Highway 101 junction.

after their ride across the Golden Gate Bridge and through Sausalito.

If you have time and are interested, you should board the Angel Island Ferry in Tiburon. The 740 acres **Angel Island** was something like the Ellis Island of the West in the last century. Between 1910 and 1940, around a million immigrants — mainly from Asia — had to stop here before they were allowed to enter the USA. Today, the island is a park that attracts many visitors on warm days with its wonderful views, a small beach, places for barbecuing, and

Across the Golden Gate Bridge and you're in the artists' settlement of Sausalito

Tiburon is even a little bit more chic than Sausalito – and its centre is considerably more clearly laid out. Many visitors rent a bicycle and enjoy an evening meal in Sam's Anchor Café *(daily | 27 Main St. | tel. 4 35 45 27 | Moderate)* or the outstanding Mexican restaurant Guayamas *(daily | 5 Main St. | tel. 4 35 63 00 | Moderate)*

a hiking path to the 240 m (787 ft) high ☆ **Mount Livermore**. On clear days, you will not only be able to see the skyline of San Francisco but also **Mount Tamalpais** and sections of **Marin County**. But, don't forget to bring food and drink with you; there are no restaurants or snack bars on the island.

TRAVEL WITH KIDS

EXPLORATORIUM
(122 C2) *(ØØ J2)*

In this interactive museum, dreamed up by scientists who are geniuses but a little bit whacky, you can touch everything and find out how it works; the almost 700 exhibits are there to be experienced hands-on. If you go to the *Tactile Dome ($20)*, you will have to find your way through a labyrinth in complete darkness. *Tue–Sun 10am–5pm | entrance fee $10–15 | 3601 Lyon St. / corner Marina Blvd. | www.exploratorium.edu | Muni 30 – Stockton*

FARALLONES VISITOR CENTER
(122 A2) *(ØØ G2)*

The Pacific Ocean lies to the west of the city – and in it, the *Gulf of the Farallones National Marine Sanctuary,* a protected area of water covering 740,000 acres. In its centre: the Farallon Islands where more seabirds breed than anywhere on the US mainland. The area is also the home of 36 marine mammals including the threatened Blue and Humpback Whale species. The visitor centre on the west side of Crissy Field promises fun for young and old: You can comb through sand to look for sharks'

teeth, stroke a sea otter's fur and feed a sea anemone. *Mon–Fri 10am–4pm | free admission |Crissy Field, Building 991 | www.farallones.org | Muni 29 – Sunset*

GOLDEN GATE FORTUNE COOKIE COMPANY ● (124 C3) *(ØØ P4)*

You will be let in on one of Chinatown's biggest secrets in this one-room factory: how fortune cookies are made. And, as long as you are here, why don't you stay a few minutes longer and listen to the hairdresser next door playing his violin. The kids will love it! *Daily 8am–8pm | free admission, $0.50 per photo | 56 Ross Alley | Muni 30 – Stockton*

SAN FRANCISCO ZOO ☺
(132 A3) *(ØØ O)*

250 animal species live in Northern California's largest zoo on the west side of the city. For only $3, you will be given a key that activates stories and information about the inhabitants in many of the cages – this also aims at encouraging visitors to protect and preserve wildlife. You will particularly enjoy a ride on the nostalgic *Dentzel Carousel ($2)* and the *Little Puffer*

The San Franciscans know how to present art and culture in a way that appeals to children and is still a lot of fun

Miniature Steam Train ($4). Daily 10am–5pm | entrance fee $9 or $15, $1 reduction with Muni ticket | I Zoo Road | www.sfzoo.org | Muni L – Traval

INSIDER TIP ▶ YODA FOUNTAIN 😊
(122 C3) (🗺 J3)
The Star Wars inventor George Lucas has established three companies in the Presidio district. The entrance is decorated with a fountain with a statue of wise Master Yoda. The lobby, as well as the park around the premises, is open to the public – this is where young and not-so-young children will find film mementos and life-sized figures including those of Darth Vader and Boba Fett. Don't forget your camera! The *Letterman Digital Arts Center* received an award from the US Green Building Council for its energy-saving measures. *Daily | free admission | 1 Letterman Dr. | Muni 28 – 19th Avenue*

YOUNG PERFORMERS THEATRE
(124 A1) (🗺 M2)
Your children will be enthralled by a visit to this theatre. It presents around 8 plays a year including classics such as *Cinderella* and *Charlie and the Chocolate Factory*. *Entrance fee $7 or $10 | Fort Mason Center, Building C, Room 300 | tel. 3 46 55 50 | www.ypt.org | Muni 30 – Stockton*

ZEUM (125 D5) (🗺 Q6)
This interactive, multimedia and technology centre aims at encouraging the creativity, as well as cooperation and communication skills, of visitors from the age of three. With their self-made videos, animated films, collages and much, much more, the Zeum does all it can to stimulate young people and their parents! *Wed–Fri 1–5pm, Sat/Sun 11am–5pm | entrance fee $8 or $10 | 221 24th St. | www.zeum.org | Muni 30 – Stockton*

FESTIVALS & EVENTS

In a hedonistic city like San Francisco – where you are always being told to have fun! – it is difficult to find a day where nothing exceptional is happening. This is a list of some of the best festivals and events. A detailed list of activities for a specific month can be found on the web under www.sfvistor.com.

EVENTS

FEBRUARY
▶ *Chinese New Year's Festival:* A gigantic parade in Chinatown with dancing dragons, bands, beauty queens and a lot of fireworks. www.chinese-parade.com

MARCH
▶ *St Patrick's Day:* Ireland's national day, is celebrated on 17 March with green beer and a parade down Market Street. www.sfstpatricksdayparade.com

APRIL
▶ *Cherry Blossom Festival:* Normally not very interesting Japantown becomes flooded with pastel colours in mid-April and pepped up with parades and artistic events
▶ *San Francisco International Film Festival:* new, mainstream and avant-garde productions www.sffs.org

MAY
▶ *Cinco de Mayo:* Mission Street celebrates Mexico's independence on 5 May
Third Sunday: Around 100,000 participants run 12½ km (7¾ mi) from the Embarcadero to the Pacific in the ▶ *Bay-to-Breakers* race. www.baytobreakers.com

JUNE
▶ ★ *Lesbian and Gay Freedom Day:* An institution in San Francisco, the colourful pageant begins at the Ferry Building and proceeds to City Hall

There are plenty of opportunities to celebrate: gay parade, jazz festival, young art and a costume competition

JULY

The ▶ INSIDER TIP *Cable Car Bell-Ringing Competition* in the middle of the month: The best single-tone-melody-ringer is elected at Union square. *www.sfmta.com*
▶ *San Francisco Marathon:* With runners from around the world. *www.thesfmarathon.com*

AUGUST

▶ *AfroSolo Arts Festival:* Local artists exhibit in various museums, galleries and theatres. *www.afrosolo.org*
▶ INSIDER TIP *Nihonmachi Street Fair:* This street festival in Japantown is celebrated with traditional food, musical and a beauty contest. *www.nihonmachistreetfair.org*

SEPTEMBER

▶ *Folsom Street Fair:* Typical of San Francisco – a lot of leather and bare skin in SoMa. *www.folsomstreetfair.com*

▶ *San Francisco Blues Festival:* The oldest blues festival in America is held in Fort Mason. *www.sfblues.com*
▶ *Jazz Festival:* A must for all jazz fans from September to November (extra concerts throughout the year). *www.sfjazz.com*

OCTOBER

▶ *Columbus Day:* At the beginning of the month, the great Italian Parade with food and drink gets underway. *www.sfcolumbusday.org*
▶ INSIDER TIP *Fleet Week:* A colourful spectacle with tours of navy ships and the world-famous Blue Angels aerobatic pilots. *www.fleetweek.us*

NOVEMBER

Christmas trees get illuminated at many locations in the city; the largest one is at Union Square. *www.unionsquare.com*

LINKS, BLOGS, APPS & MORE

LINKS

▶ www.7x7.com Web version of the glossy, stylish 7X7 magazine that gives the most up-to-date news about restaurants, bars and cultural events

▶ www.onlyinsanfrancisco.com/calendar What's happening and where? The tourist office provides the answers organised by the districts of the city

▶ www.sfmuseum.org A virtual city museum with many exhibitions including one on the 1849 Gold Rush and another on the history of rock music in the Bay Area

▶ www.baycitizen.org Independent web newspaper in which prize-winning journalists have reported on the Bay Area, without mincing their words, since 2010

BLOGS & FORUMS

▶ www.twitter.com/michaelbauer1 and insidescoopsf.sfgate.com San Francisco's famous restaurant critic Michael Bauer tests newcomers and classics

▶ www.pacoandbetty.com/blog The photographer couple Whitney and Marcellos Parker portray people and animals in front of the most fascinating backdrops of the city

▶ sf.streetsblog.org and bikescape.blogspot.com What is up on San Francisco's streets and cycle paths?

▶ www.twitter.com/austinat The author of this guide book twitters – verbally and visually – about the country and the people living there

APPS

▶ San Franciscans love their iPhones almost as much as their public transport system. This is made easier using the BART and Caltrain apps. And, Routesy even combines the lines of several transport services

Regardless of whether you are still preparing your trip or already in San Francisco: these addresses will provide you with more information, videos and networks to make your holiday even more enjoyable

▶ Where is the next In-N-Out-Burger? The app of this name for iPhone and Android owners can tell you. And, if you want to know which restaurants, bars and shops can be found nearby, just consult the extremely useful Yelp app

▶ sanfranciscopoetry.blip.tv John Rhodes and Clara Hsu present local authors and musicians in their San Francisco Open Mic Poetry Podcast

▶ www.youtube.com/user/Sam Crayne The photographer Sam Crayne's camera invests everyday life in San Francisco with the charm of a fairytale

▶ www.thebaybridged.com/podcasts All the news on San Francisco's vibrant music scene

▶ www.youtube.com/watch?v=pnDjmNNC9So and www.youtube.com/watch? v=Vqcz_tllnwM A fascinating trip down Market Street in 1900 and again in 2005

▶ www.youtube.com/watch?v=1DseqKdOMtM Philip Bloom was one of the first photographers to use a single-lens reflex camera as a film camera for 'San Francisco's People'

▶ sfbay.craigslist.org No matter whether you want to catch a lift somewhere, are looking for a place to stay, clothing or things for the home – you will find it all on Craigslist

▶ www.yelp.com Yelper started its rise to fame in San Francisco: completely normal people write amusing, and sometimes wicked, criticisms of shops, hairdressers, cafés and restaurants all through the day

▶ www.airbnb.com Would you like to spend some time in a Victorian house or minimalist loft? Quite a few San Franciscans will let you stay with them for a few dollars a night – you can occasionally even find an entire flat for less than $100

TRAVEL TIPS

ARRIVAL

✈ Scheduled flights from overseas, as well as charters, land at *San Francisco International Airport (SFO)* 16 miles south of Downtown. There are several ways to reach the inner city.

Buses: The *Super Shuttle* departs from the airport for the centre of town almost every twenty minutes throughout the day. Price: $17. The public *Sam Trans Bus* goes to the Transbay terminal at the corner of Howard and Main Street in the Downtown area: Route KX. One big drawback: only hand luggage is allowed. Price: $5 or $2.50

Taxis: The fare to Downtown is around $40.

Rented cars: The Blue Line of the fully automatic, free *AirTrans* will take you to the hire car centre in 15 minutes, 24 hours a day.

Bart Rapid Transport: There is also a rail connection between the airport and the centre of town. The fare from the terminal is currently about $8. Up-to-date schedules and iPhone app under: *www.bart.gov*.

🚌 The long-distance *Greyhound/Trailways* buses arrive at the Transbay terminal at the corner of Howard and Main Street.

🚗 From the south: Via US Highway 101 or Interstate I-380, by I-5 to I-580 and I-80, by Route 1 direct. From the east: I-580 or I-80 to the Bay Bridge. From the north: US 101 to the Golden Gate Bridge.

CUSTOMS

The following goods can be imported duty-free into the USA: 1 litre of alcohol over 22 percent, 200 cigarettes and gifts up to a value of $100. It is forbidden to bring vegetables, fruit, meat and milk with you.

The following goods can be imported duty-free into the EU: 1 litre of alcohol over 22 percent or 2 litres of wine, 200 cigarettes, 50g of perfume or 250g of eau de toilette and other goods up to a value of 390 pounds/430 euros.

CURRENCY

1 dollar = 100 cents. Notes *(bills)* – 1, 2, 5, 10, 20 and 100 dollars. Coins: *penny* (1 cent), *nickel* (5 cents), *dime* (10 cents), *quarter* (25 cents), *buck* (1 dollar).

The most popular way to pay is with a credit card (American Express, MasterCard, Visa). It is also possible to use cash dispensers with an EC card. Travellers cheques are accepted everywhere as a means of payment and you will receive change in cash. Foreign currencies can be exchanged

---

RESPONSIBLE TRAVEL

It doesn't take a lot to be environmentally friendly whilst travelling. Don't just think about your carbon footprint whilst flying to and from your holiday destination but also about how you can protect nature and culture abroad. As a tourist it is especially important to respect nature, look out for local products, cycle instead of driving, save water and much more. If you would like to find out more about eco-tourism please visit: *www.ecotourism.org*

at the airport, in hotels and in large banks but the rates are poor. Many small shops do not accept notes of more then $20, so be sure to ask for small denominations when you change.

DRIVING

Car-rental companies have offices at the airport and at many locations in the city. You require a driving license and credit card. Even if you pay by voucher, a credit card is required as a security measure. Traffic regulations: it is compulsory to wear seatbelts. The blood alcohol limit is 0.8. If you stop at a red traffic light, you can still turn right. Cable cars always have right-of-way; so do pedestrians.

Parking is strictly forbidden at bus stops and in front of fire hydrants. Everything else is regulated by marks on the kerb. Red: no stopping. Yellow: loading area for deliveries. Green 10-minute parking during business hours. The already very high parking fees continue to rise and now many parking meters even accept credit cards.

Hotels often charge as much as $40 or $50 a night for parking – this makes it worthwhile to look for a guarded car park or a parking space on the street on your own; *sanfrancisco.bestparking.com* can help you with this. Be careful: if your vehicle hinders a bus in the rush hour, or the street cleaners in the early morning, you will be severely fined or the car might even be towed away. Pay attention to the signs on the roadside!

ELECTRICITY

You will need an adapter for American power points and your electrical equipment must be able to operate at 110 volts and 60 hertz.

BUDGETING

Snack	$7.50
	for a sandwich
Wine	$7–9.50
	for a glass
Caffè latte	$3.80
	for a medium cup
Postcard	$1.25
	for a postcard and postage
Jeans	$40–48
	for Levi's 501
Cable car	$6
	for a single trip

EMBASSIES & CONSULATES

BRITISH CONSULATE-GENERAL
1 Sansome Street | Suite 850 | San Francisco, CA 94104 | tel. (415) 617 1300 | ukinusa.fco.gov.uk/en/about-us/other-locations/sf

CONSULATE-GENERAL OF CANADA
580 California Street | 14th floor | San Francisco, CA 94104 | tel. (415) 834 3180 | www.canadainternational.gc.ca/san_francisco

CONSULATE-GENERAL OF IRELAND
100 Pine Street | Suite 3350 | San Francisco, CA 94111 | tel. (415) 392 4214 | www.consulateofirelandsanfrancisco.org/home/index.aspx?id=35625

EMERGENCY SERVICES

Emergencies of all kinds: tel. 911
Ambulance: tel. 9 31 39 00
Police: tel. 5 53 01 23
or: 0 for the operator

IMMIGRATION

People entering the country need a machine-readable passport (applies to children as well) and must register online before arrival: *https://esta.cbp.dhs.gov/esta*. An entry charge of $14, which can only be paid by credit card, is due for this service. If you do not have a credit card yourself, a third party can take care of this on your behalf. If you intend to stay for longer than three months, you require a visa. Make sure to inform yourself of the latest requirements; one possibility is on the internet under *www.dhs.gov*.

INFORMATION BEFORE YOU DEPART

DISCOVER AMERICA
The official travel and tourism website of the USA can probably answer most of your questions and also includes interactive maps: *www.discover.america.com*

INFORMATION IN SAN FRANCISCO

SAN FRANCISCO CONVENTION & VISITORS BUREAU
(124 C5) (*P6*) The Bureau is located on the lower level of the Hallidie Plaza at the corner of Powell and Market St. *(900 Market St. | San Francisco, CA 94102 | tel. 3 91 20 00 | www.sfvisitor.org)*.

VISIT USA COMMITTEE UK
This is a non-governmental union of travel and tourism experts that provides a great deal of useful information about airlines, hotel chains, tour operators, car hire companies, the individual states, regions and cities of the USA, as well as the latest entry regulations on its website *www.visitusa.org.uk*

INTERNET CAFÉS & WIFI

San Francisco is considered the internet capital of the USA – however, a free WiFi connection for the entire city has never really got going. Internet access is available free of charge at the airport and in most cafés. Hotels often charge a daily rate. If you want to save money, you can go online in the *Apple Store (1 Stockton St.)* or at one of the terminals in the *Public Library (100 Larkin St.)*. The most popular internet cafés in the city with free WiFi are:
– *The Quetzal*, roasts its own coffee and serves delicious breakfast *(1234 Polk St.)*
– *@ maximos*, more tourists but tasty smoothies and salads *(180 Seventh St.)*
– *Camille's Sidewalk Café*, good sandwiches and wraps *(One Market Plaza, 30 Mission St.)*

MEDICAL SERVICES

Saint Francis Memorial Hospital *(900 Hyde St. | tel. 3 53 60 00)* and the San Francisco Medical Society *(tel. 5 61 08 50)* can provide information on doctors (as well as those who speak other languages, if needed); the San Francisco Dental Society *(tel. 9 28 73 37)* offers the same service for dentists.
The *Emergency Room* in the hospitals is clearly signed and you will be helped there in acute cases. It is usual for staff to ask for a credit card before giving treatment. Most accept MasterCard and Visa. But, in any case, be sure to take out foreign travel health insurance before leaving home.

OPENING HOURS

There are virtually no restrictions on opening hours in San Francisco; many shops do not even close on the most important public holidays.

PERSONAL SAFETY

As in any American city, there are certain districts and blocks in San Francisco that it is better to avoid. You really don't have to go on an excursion to the Tenderloin section north of the Civic Center. You should also stay away from the areas in the Western Addition between Van Ness Avenue and Fillmore Street. This is where you will find the *housing projects*, fenced-in blocks of flats where there is frequently unrest.

PHONES & MOBILE PHONES

Local calls cost 50 cents. It is best to use telephones where you can pay using a credit card for long distance calls. The most inexpensive possibility is with *prepaid phone cards* that are available in drugstores, petrol stations and supermarkets. For long distance calls, dial 1 + area code (three digits) + seven-digit number. Country codes for calling from the USA (011 + 44 for the UK) followed by the local area code (without 0) and the number. If you have a triple-band mobile phone that supports the American 1900 MHz frequency, you should consider buying a *prepaid Globalsim SIM card*. It is cheaper than the expensive roaming fees charged by many European mobile-phone companies.

To reach the telephone numbers listed in this book from outside the USA, dial the codes for the USA and San Francisco *001 415* followed by the seven-digit number.

CURRENCY CONVERTER

$	£	£	$
1	0.70	1	1.40
3	2.10	3	4.20
5	3.50	5	7
13	9.10	13	18.20
40	28	40	56
75	52.50	75	105
120	84	120	168
250	175	250	350
500	350	500	700

For current exchange rates see www.xe.com

POST

Post offices are open Mon–Fri 9am–5pm, larger ones also Sat 8.30am–noon. The postage for airmail letters and postcards to Europe is 98 cents.

PUBLIC TRANSPORT

San Francisco is very proud of its well-developed transport network. The system is made up of four components:
Cable Car: the cable cars travel on three routes: Powell–Hyde, Powell–Mason and California Street.
Muni Bus: buses provide the best means of public transport in the inner city. Ask the bus driver where you should get off. White letters on a black ground on the sign at the front of the bus: *Local Service* – halts at all stops. Red on white: *Express* – only during the rush hour and does not stop everywhere. White on Green: *Limited* – does not stop everywhere.
Muni Metro: trams that run partly under and partly above the ground. The lines all travel down Market St. but then branch out towards the south-west. You can save

money with a INSIDER TIP *Muni Pass* valid for 1, 3 or 7 days or one month. The passes can be bought in the airport's entrance hall and at many other locations *(info: www.sfmta.com/cms/mfares/passvend.htm | tel. 311 (only in SF), 7012311).*

Bart: a rapid transport system between Daly City and Oakland that connects San Francisco with the East Bay and airport.

TAXIS

Prices: $3.10 basic charge plus $2.25 per mile. Drivers expect to be tipped. *Telephone reservations Arrow Cab: tel. 6433181 | Desoto Cab Co: tel. 9701300 | Veteran's Cab: tel. 5521300 | Yellow cab: tel. 333 3333*

TIME

San Francisco is in the *Pacific Time Zone*: Greenwich Mean Time – 8 hours. The start and end of daylight saving time varies; it is currently from the last Sunday in March until the first Sunday in November.

TIPPING

Everybody who provides a service lives almost exclusively from tips: barkeeper: $1 per drink, bellboy: $2–5, waiter: 15–20 percent, porter: at least $1 per piece of luggage, valet (parking attendant): $1–2 for parking and collecting the car, maid: $2–5 a day.

TOURS

ON TWO TO SIX WHEELS

The 3½-hour tour offered by *All San Francisco Tours ($46 | www.allsanfrancisco tours.com)* takes you to the most important sights in town. A 'hop-on-hop-off' tour in a double-decker bus ($28) makes it possible for you to explore San Francisco

at your own pace. *Extranomical Adventures (www.extranomical.com)* offers a similar tour with a ticket ($39) that is valid for two days.

Something out of the ordinary: the six-wheel amphibious vehicles operated by *Ride the Ducks ($32 | sanfrancisco.ridethe ducks.com)* with which you can discover all that North Beach, Downtown and Fisherman's Wharf have to offer from the land and from the water. INSIDER TIP *Mr. Toads Tours (www.mrtoadstours.com)* is a more personal operation – the family business uses vintage cars (from $36).

Do you want to get behind the steering wheel yourself? Then the three-wheel *GoCar (www.gocartours.com | from $49)* could be perfect for you. One or two people can travel through the city, guided by GPS navigation, in the bright yellow, roadworthy open metal crates. If four or three wheels are too many for you, you can try a futuristic *Segway Scooter ($70 | www.citysegwaytours.com)* and scare the wits out of people around Fisherman's Wharf and North Beach.

FOR PEDESTRIANS

Free insider tours? The ● *San Francisco City Guides* are local fans of their city who will make you acquainted with the art déco buildings in the Marina, murals in the Mission and the history of earthquakes in the inner city. It is not necessary to book in advance; up-to-date information is available under *www.sfcityguides.org*.

Two tours are devoted to the city's Victorian buildings: the Haight-Ashbury Walking Tour *($20 | www.haightashburytour.com)* and the Victorian Home Walk *($25 | www.victorianwalk.com)*. The latter even takes you to parts of the city that are closed to tour buses.

The *San Francisco Ghost Hunt ($20 | www.sfghost-hunt.com)* is a mixture of horror and history during which you will hunt down ghosts in old hotels and Victorian houses. The *SF Vampire Tour ($20 | www.sfvampiretour.com)* on Nob Hill is based to 85% on fact – it's up to you to find out about the remaining 15%.

WEIGHTS & MEASURES

In America the same system of measurement is used as in the UK (i.e inch, foot, yard, mile). With regard to weights, up to and including the pound, the two systems are the same. The Americans never use the stone as a weight. The hundredweight (cwt) in England is always 112 pounds, or 8 stone. In the US, the hundredweight is 100 lb. Liquid measures: the gallon in use in the US is the old 'Queen Anne' gallon, of 1707 (231 in^3). The Imperial gallon is bigger at 277.4 in^3. As there are 8 pints to the gallon, the pint is different in the two systems. In the US there are 16 fl. oz. to the pint, the Imperial has 20, so the two fluid ounces are very close. Clothing sizes differ too, especially in the case of women's clothing. As a rule of thumb, the following standard clothing sizes are a useful guideline. For men's clothing, the same system is used in the USA as in the UK.

WOMEN'S CLOTHING SIZES

USA	6	8	10	12	14
UK	8	10	12	14	16

MEN'S CLOTHING SIZES (SUITS, SWEATERS, ETC.)

UK/US	38	40	42	44	46	48	50	52	54
EU	48	50	52	54	56	58	60	62	64

WEATHER IN SAN FRANCISCO

	Jan	Feb	March	April	May	June	July	Aug	Sept	Oct	Nov	Dec
Daytime temperatures in °C/°F	13/55	15/59	16/61	17/63	17/63	18/64	18/64	186/64	20/68	20/68	18/64	14/57
Nighttime temperatures in °C/°F	7/45	8/46	9/48	10/50	11/52	12/54	12/54	12/54	13/55	12/54	10/50	8/46
Sunshine hours/day	5	7	8	9	10	11	9	8	9	8	6	5
Precipitation days/month	8	7	8	6	2	1	0	0	0	2	7	8
Water temperatures in °C/°F	11/52	11/52	12/54	12/54	13/55	14/54	15/59	15/59	16/61	15/59	13/55	11/52

NOTES

*Check listings on web

Places we Want to Go

Alcatraz / Clam Chowder Fisherman's Wharf.
Trolley car - 'Cable car'
Castro   'Twin Peaks) + theatre/film *
Golden Gate Park. / Haight Ashbury.
Chinatown (Jap T Garden) Northern Lights Book Shop-
Art galleries. C - Legion of honor
                k. SOMA

Aquarium?

Places we Want to eat

Chinatown.

FOR YOUR NEXT HOLIDAY ...

MARCO POLO TRAVEL GUIDES

MARCO POLO
With ROAD ATLAS & PULL-OUT MAP
LAKE GARDA
T SALÒ WITH MOUNTAIN BIKE
Malcesine takes bikes too
SSES" IN SALÒ
ate ..bocetti
Travel with Insider Tips

MARCO POLO
With STREET ATLAS & PULL-OUT MAP
NEW YORK
OWS, WILD FLOWERS AND SKYSCRAPERS
chic: the High Line in Chelsea
AIL ON CLOUD NINE
op bar at 230 Fifth Street
Travel with Insider Tips

MARCO POLO
With ROAD ATLAS & PULL-OUT MAP
FRENCH RIVIERA
NICE, CANNES & MONACO
SPECTACULAR GRAND CANYON DU VERDON
Breath-taking scenery that takes some beating
SNIFFING THE AIR
The perfume manufacturers of Grasse
Travel with Insider Tips

MARCO POLO
With ROAD ATLAS & PULL-OUT MAP
ALLORCA
AN FLAIR IN THE MEDITERRANEAN
Mallorca's most beautiful beach
E..IN" CROWD MEET
Tenda in Deià
Travel with Insider Tips

MARCO POLO
With STREET ATLAS & PULL-OUT MAP
BERLIN
A STUNNING ISLAND JUST FOR ART
Showcasing treasures from around the world
STAY COOL AT NIGHT
scene sets the trend
Travel with Insider Tips

www.marcopolouk.com

- PACKED WITH INSIDER TIPS
- BEST WALKS AND TOURS
- FULL-COLOUR PULL-OUT MAP
  AND STREET ATLAS

STREET ATLAS

The green line ▬▬▬ indicates the Walking tours (p. 98–103)

All tours are also marked on the pull-out map

Photo: Financial Disttrict

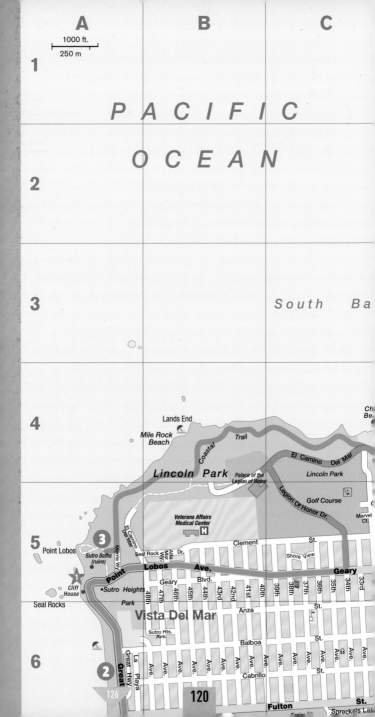

A **B** **C**

1

1000 ft.
250 m

P A C I F I C

O C E A N

2

3

South   Ba

Ch
Be

4

Lands End

Mile Rock
Beach

Coastal   Trail

El Camino   Del Mar

Lincoln Park

Palace of the
Legion of Honor

Lincoln Park
Golf Course

Legion Of Honor Dr.

Marvel
Ct

5

Point Lobos

③

Sutro Baths
(ruins)

El Camino Del Mar

Merrie Wy.

Seal Rock

Alta Mar Dr.

Veterans Affairs
Medical Center
H

Clement   St.

Shore View

Point

Lobos   Ave.

Geary

Cliff
House

•Sutro Heights
Park

Geary   Blvd.

48th
47th
46th
45th
44th
43rd
42nd
41st
40th
39th
38th
37th
36th
35th
34th
33rd

Seal Rocks

Vista Del Mar

Sutro Hts.
Ave.

Anza   St.

Balboa   St.

6

La
Playa

Great Hwy

② 126

Great

Cabrillo   Ave.

Fulton   St.

120

Spreckels Lake

Senior

D E F

4 E Fort Point
National Historic
Site

Golden
Gate
2 Bridge
(Toll)

1 **2**

Marine Dr.

1

Battery

3

101

E. Rd. Lincoln

Long Ave.

1 Pearce St.

Marine Dr

Hoffman St.

E. Armstead Rd.

4

Crissy Field

Crissy Blvd.

Field

2

Battery

Merchant Rd.

Storey Ave.

Stone St.

Miller Rd.

Battery Blaney Rd.

Battery Caulfield Rd.

Wagner Rd.

Cowles St.

Patten Ave.

McDowell Ave.

Ruckman Ave.

San
Francisco
National
Cemetery

Kinzey St.

Ralston Ave.

Union

Simonds Loop

Liggett Ave.

Upton Ave.

1

Kobbe

Bivd

Harrison

Hitchcock

Wright

3

2

P r e s i d i o

(Golden Gate Nat'l
Recreation Area)

Park
Amatury
Loop

Washington

Nauman

Baker
Beach

Washington

Compton Rd.

Blvd.

Maple
Rd

3

Pershing

Stilwell

Dr.

Battery Caulfield Rd.

Gen. Douglas MacArthur
(Tunnel)

Presidio

Golf

Course

Battery Chamberlin Rd.

Bowley St.

Lincoln

Brooks St.

Baker Ct.

Public Health
Service Hospital

H

Mountain
Lake

4

Gibson Rd.

Scenic Wy.

Ave.

25th Ave.

2

Seacliff

Howard Rd.

Mountain Lake Park

Presidi

McLaren
Ave.

Seacliff

25th

West Clay

Lake St.

N. 15th Ave.

Lake St.

ake

St.

St.

St.

St.

California

St.

California St.

California

St.

St.

Clement

Clement

5

Tacoma
St.

Blvd.

30th 29th 28th 27th 26th 25th 24th 23rd 22nd 21st 20th 19th 18th 17th 16th 15th 14th

Geary Blvd.

12th 11th 10th 9th 8th 7th 6th

Funston

Anza

Anza

Richmond

Park Presidio

Balboa

Balboa

St.

Ave.

Ave.

Ave.

Ave.

Ave.

Ave.

Ave.

St.

Cabrillo

Cabrillo

Granat
Ct.

6

rge
shington
hschool

Ave.

Ave.

Ave.

Ave.

Fulton St.

121

By-Pass

Dr.

127

2

Ful

Cross Over Dr.

Park

Kenn

John F. K

Dr.

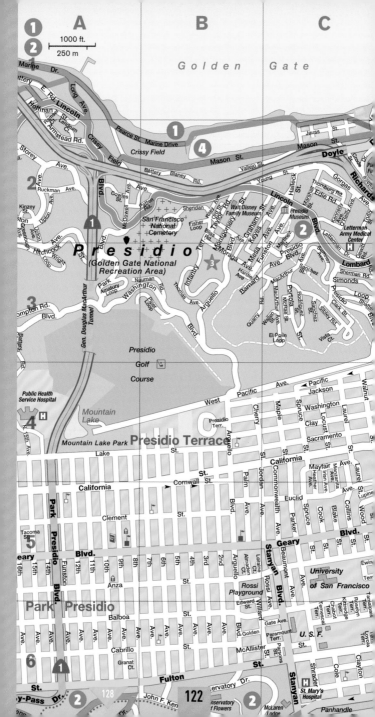

A B C

1
2

1000 ft.
250 m

Golden   Gate

Marine Dr.

E. Rd. Long Ave.
Battery

Hoffman **Lincoln**
Rimlon
Langum
Ramero

Armstead Rd. Crissy

Pearce St. Marine Drive **1**

4

Crissy Field

Mason St.

Jauss St.

Mason **Doyle**

Richards

Storey Ave.

2 Ruckman Ave.

Cowles Ave.
St. Fulton

McDowell
Ave.

Battery Blaney Rd.

Vallejo St.

Young St.

Lincoln

Halleck St.

Thornburg Rd. Edie Rd.

Gorgas

2

Kinzey
St.
Upton
Ave.
Greenough
Hitchcock
Loop

Park

Blvd.

Sheridan

Fisher
Loop

1

**San Francisco
National
Cemetery**

Taylor Rd.

Graham

Moraga

Montgomery

Walt Disney
Family Museum

Keyes

Funston

Presidio

St.

Presidio
Museum

Edie Rd.

Letterman **2**

Letterman
Army Medical
Center

Wright
Ave.

P r e s i d i o
*(Golden Gate National
Recreation Area)*

3

Mesa

Hardie
Ave.

Barnard

Presidio

Blvd.

MacArthur

Sumner

Sanches Ave.

Lombard

Sherman Rd.

Simonds

3
Compton Rd.
Blvd.

Battery

Gen. Douglas MacArthur
Tunnel

Washington

Amatury
Loop

Nauman

Paul
Loop

Thomas

Infantry

Arguello

Ave.

Portola

MacArthur

McRae St.

Rodriguez

Quarry

Walton

El Polin
Loop

St.

Sanches

Sibley Rd.

Clark St.

Vista Ct.

Loop
Shafter

Blvd.

*Presidio
Golf
Course*

**Public Health
Service Hospital**

4 H

**Mountain
Lake**

Pacific Ave. ◄ Pacific
Jackson

West

Washington

Maple

Cherry

Spruce

Laurel

Locust

Walnut

Mountain Lake Park **Presidio Terrace**

Presidio
Terr.

Clay

Sacramento

California

Washington

Clay

Laurel

Lake

Arguello

St.

Mayfair Ave.

Heather Ave.
Ave.

Iron Ave.

Manzanita
Ave.

N. 15th Ave.

California

Cornwall St.

Palm

Jordan

Commonwealth

Ave.

Ave.

Euclid Ave.

Spruce

Parker

Cook

Blake

Collins

St.

Wood

Lupine

Laurel

Clement

St.

St.

St.

St.

St.

St.

St.

Tacoma
St.

5

Geary

Blvd.

9th 8th 7th 6th 5th 4th 3rd 2nd

Anza

Park

Presidio

Blvd.

12th 11th 10th

Arguello

Almaden

Loraine
Ct.

Rossi
Playground

Stanyan

Beaumont
Ave.

Rossi Ave.

Willard

Edward
St.

**University
of San Francisco**

Ewing
Terr.

Anglo
Terr.

Rossiyn
Terr.

Chabot
Terr.

Kittredge
Terr.

Terr.

Park **Presidio**

16th 15th 14th

Balboa

Cabrillo

Ave. Ave. Ave. Ave. Ave.

St.

Arguello

Blvd.

Gate Ave.

Paramount
Terr.

Golden

Pierce St.

U. S. F.

Loyola
Terr.

Ave.

Clayton

6 **1**

Granat
Ct.

McAllister

St.

Stanyan

Shrader

Cole

St.

128

Fulton

122

nservatory Dr.

John F. Ken

f Flowers

2

McLaren
Lodge

H

**St. Mary's
Hospital**

Panhandle

y-Pass **2**

Dr.

enn

1000 ft.
250 m

San Francisco Bay

31

29

27

23 19

17

Greenwich St. 15

Napier F 7
Union St. F 1
Commerce St. 9
Davis

Fishing Pier

North Beach

Broadway 3

F

S.G. Walton Sq.
Jackson St.
Battery Michele 1
Sansome Jackson St.
Maritime 2
Plaza Embarcadero
Mark Twain Merchant Center
Clay St.

to Tiburon, Vallejo, Sausalito, Larkspur

to East Bay
BART Trans-Bay Tube

to Alameda

to Harbor Bay Isle

2

3

Justin
Herman
Plaza

World Trade
Center/Ferry
Building

1

F 15

Commercial St.
Halleck
Sacramento Commercial Front St.
101 California
St. Buld'g
Treasury F
Market St.
Embarcadero F
F
Rincon
Center
Clay St.
Montgomery

2 Embarcadero

F Spear St.

2

City Front
District
Folsom & The
Embarcadero

Steuart

Fremont St.
1st St.
Stevenson St.
New
Stevenson St.
Minna St.
Natoma St.
Howard Beale St.
Main St.
Spear St.
Zeno Pl.

Pier 24

San Francisco – Oakland Bay Bridge [Toll]

Pier 26

temp. Transbay
Transit Terminal

Pier 28

South of
Market

Cartoon Art
Museum
9
Museum of
Modern Art
Yerba Buena
Gardens
retreon
Zeum
Moscone
Center

Folsom St.
Tehama St.
Clementina St.
Dow Pl.
Clementina St.
Guy Pl.
Lansing St.
Hawthorne St.
Harrison St.
Bayside Village

The Embarcadero

Pier 30

2

(SoMa)

3rd

Bryant St.
Stillman St.
Federal St.
Colin P. Kelly Jr. St.
Boardman Pl.
Welsh St.
Vermont
South
Beach

Pier 34

Brannan & The
Embarcadero

Pier 36

Pier 38

80

Stanford St.
Tabor Ct.
SouthPark
Verona Pl.
2nd St.
Clarence Pl.
Decker St.
De Boom St.
Rollin P.

Pier 40

South
Beach
Harbor

5

Shipley St.
Clara St.
3rd St.
Zoe St.
Ritch St.

King St.

2nd & King St.

AT & T Park

Willie
Mays Plaza

Welsh St.
Freelon St.
Clyde
Brannan St.
4th St.
Bluxome St.
Townsend

Caltrain St.

Berry St.

2

Berry St.

4th & King St.

Channel St.

3rd

Terry A. Francois Blvd.

Pier 48

6

6th St.
Harriet St.
Boardman Pl.
Morris St.

Pier 50
Mission
Rock
Terminal

Concourse
xhibition Center
Townsend

125

131

4th St.

Pier
52

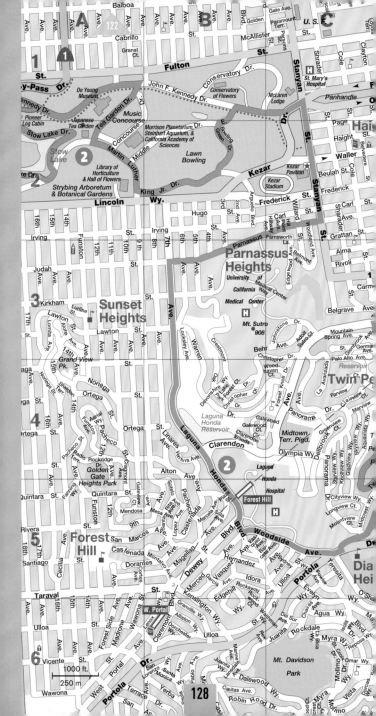

A
B
C

Balboa
Ave.
Ave.
Ave.

Gate Ave.
Golden
Paramount Terr.
U.S.C

1
St.
Cabrillo
Granat Ct.

McAllister
St.
Parsons
St.

Clayton
Cole
Terr.

Fulton
St.

Shrader
St.
St. Mary's
Hospital

Conservatory
Dr.
John F. Kennedy Dr.
Conservatory
of Flowers
McLaren
Lodge

Panhandle

De Young
Museum

Page
St.

Hai

y-Pass Dr.
Kennedy Dr.

Music
Concourse

Haight
St.

Belvedere

Pioneer
Log Cabin
Japanese
Tea Garden
Tea Garden Dr.

Morrison Planetarium Dr.
Steinhart Aquarium, &
California Academy of
Sciences

Waller
St.

Stow Lake Dr.
Concourse

E.
Green
Dr.

Beulah St.
Cole

2
Stow
Lake

Library of
Horticulture
& Hall of Flowers
Strybing Arboretum
& Botanical Gardens

Martin Luther
Middle

Lawn
Bowling

Kezar
St.

Kezar
Pavilion

Frederick

re Dr.

King
Jr.
Wy.

Kezar
Stadium

Lincoln
Wy.

Arguello Blvd.
3rd
2nd
Ave.

Frederick
St.

Stanyan
St.

16th
15th
14th
St.

Hugo
St.

Irving
7th
6th
5th
4th

Parnassus
Farnsworth
La.

Carl
St.

Grattan
St.

Irving
St.

Funston
12th
11th
10th
9th
8th
Ave.
St.

**Parnassus
Heights**

Carl
Palm
Hillway
Ave.
Woodland Ave.

Sharader
Ave.
St.

Judah
Ave.

University of
California
Medical Center

Belmont
Ave.
Edgewood
Ave.

Alma
St.

Rivoli
St.

3
Kirkham
St.

Lurline
St.

**Sunset
Heights**

Lawton
St.

Medical Center

Carme

17th
Lomita
Aloha
Ave.
14th
St.

Lawton
St.
Ave.
Ave.

Locksley
Warren
Crestmont

Mt. Sutro
908

Johnstone
Dr.

Belgrave
Ave.

Grand View
Pk.
15th

Behr
Ave.

Adolf
Sutro Ct.

Mountain
Spring Ave.

aga
Ave.
Noriega
Shelton
Terr.
14th

Ortega
St.

Christopher
Dr.
Wood-
haven
Ct.

Palo Alto Ave.
St.
Gumbookk
Ave.
Germain

ega
St.
16th

Devonshire Wy.
Oak
Forest
Park
Forest
Dr.
Christopher Dr.

Forest
Knoll
Dr.

Fairview
St.

Twin Pe

4
rtega

Aerial
Funston
Lake
St.
Pacheco
12th
St.

Ortega

Linares
Ave.
Ventura Ave.

Laguna Honda
Reservoir

Galewood
Ct.
Clarendon
Woods

Panorama
Dr.

Clairview
Ct.
Greenview
Ct.
Marview

Pacheco
Radio
Dr.
Rockridge

Clarendon

Midtown
Terr. Plgd.

Dellbrook
Ave.

Aquavista

Golden
Gate
Heights Park

Cragmont
Ave.

Alton
Ave.

Olympia Wy.

Crestline
Ave.

Quintara
St.
Quintara
St.

Lagunda
Honda

Cityview Wy.

Funston
12th
Ave.

Mendosa
Ave.
9th
Rio
Ave.
Lopez
Marcela Ave.
Lola
Ave.

Hospital

Forest Hill
H

Longview Ct.

Mounviview
Ct.

Midcrest Wy.

5
Rivera
St.

**Forest
Hill**

San Marcos
Ave.

Castenada
Ave.

Magellan
Ave.

Hernandez
Ave.

Idora
Ave.

Woodside
Ave.

Portola

Di
Hei

17th
18th
Santiago
St.

Cecilia
Ave.
Castenada
St.

Dorantes
Ave.
Montalvo
Ave.
Cortes
Ave.

Dewey
Merced

Rockaway
Rock

Ulloa
Ave.

Teresita

O'She

Taraval
St.

15th
14th
Ave.

Forest Side
Ave.
Madrone
Ave.
Wawona
St.
Lenox

Kensington Wy.
Granville Wy.
Alliston Wy.
Edgehill
Way

Del Sur
Charles
Wy.
Evelyn
Wy.

Agua Wy.

6
Vicente
St.
Ulloa
St.

Ave.
Ave.
Ave.

W. Portal

Claremont
Dorchester
Ulloa

Juanita
Wy.

Rockdale
Dr.
La Bica
Reposa Wy.
Myra Wy.

1000 ft.
250 m

West
Portal
San
Lorenzo
Santa
Monica
Pablo
Yerba

Juanita
Wy.

**Mt. Davidson
Park**

Omar Wy.
Vista

Wawona
Portola
Dr.
Terrace
San

128

Casitas Ave.
Dalewood
Wy.

Robin Hood Dr.

Grid references: A, B, C (top); 1, 2, 3, 4, 5, 6 (left side)

Notable labels include:
- Van Ness
- Market St.
- South Van Ness Ave.
- U.C. Extension Center
- Church St.
- Mission Dolores
- Mission Park
- Dolores Heights
- Mission
- Franklin Square
- Potrero Ave.
- Cesar Chavez (Army)
- St. Luke's Hospital
- Bernal Heights
- Bernal Hts. Pk.
- Glen Park
- 101

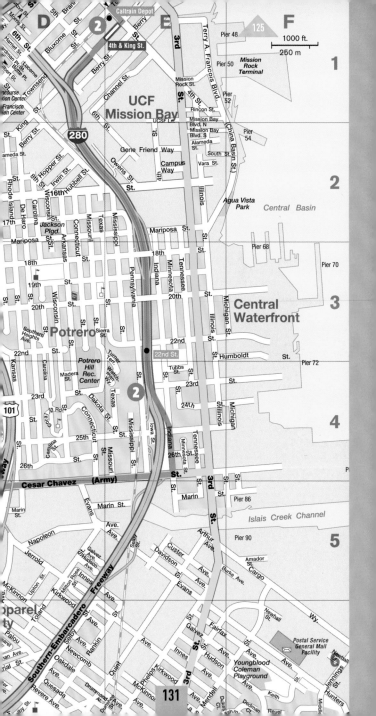

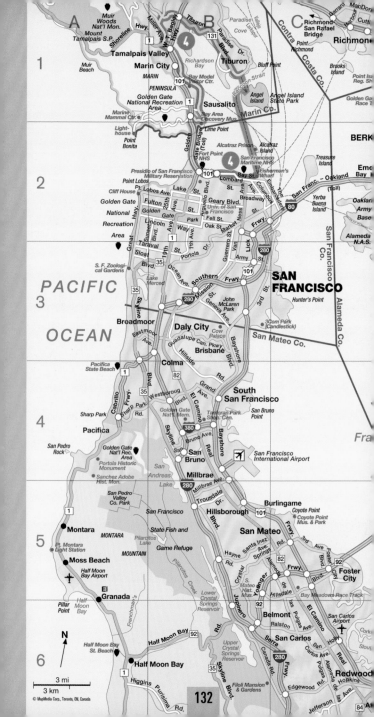

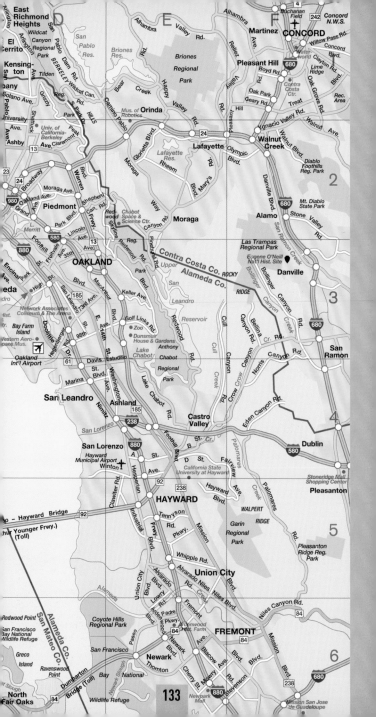

This index lists a selection of the streets and squares shown in the street atlas

Ave = Avenue
Blvd = Boulevard
St = Street

KEY TO STREET ATLAS

Expressway		Municipal Boundary	
Toll Expressway		Community Centre	
Highway		Shopping Centre	
80 Interstate Highway Number		Liquor Store	
101 U. S. Highway Number		Hotel/Motel	
1 State Highway Number		*VICTO* Shopping District	
Arterial Road		Fire Hall	
One Way Street		Police Station	
Railway		Hospital	
Paul Ave. Caltrain Station		Post Office	
BART Line		City or Town Hall	
Powell St. BART Station		Travel Information	
Cable Car		Court House	
Historic Streetcar		Bus Terminal	
MUNI Metro Line		Palace of Worship	
Church MUNI Metro Station		Public Library	
Beach		Live Theatre or Concert Hall	
Marina		Museum or Art Gallery	
National Park		Cinema	
Other Park		Monument/Public Art	
Golf Course		Winery	
Cemetery		Public Elementary School	
Walking Trail		Public Secondary School	
Bicycle Path		Parochial Elementary School	
Campground		Parochial Secondary School	
Outdoor Swimming Pool		Private School	
Indoor Swimming Pool		College	
Tennis Court		Walking tours	
		MARCO POLO Highlight	

INDEX

This index lists all places and sights, plus the names of important people featured in this guide. Numbers in bold indicate a main entry.

CREDITS

WRITE TO US

e-mail: info@marcopologuides.co.uk

Did you have a great holiday?
Is there something on your mind?
Whatever it is, let us know!
Whether you want to praise, alert us
to errors or give us a personal tip –
MARCO POLO would be pleased to
hear from you.
We do everything we can to provide the
very latest information for your trip.

Nevertheless, despite all of our authors'
thorough research, errors can creep in.
MARCO POLO does not accept any
liability for this. Please contact us by
e-mail or post.

MARCO POLO Travel Publishing Ltd
Pinewood, Chineham Business Park
Crockford Lane, Chineham
Basingstoke, Hampshire RG24 8AL
United Kingdom

PICTURE CREDITS
Cover photograph: Golden Gate Bridge (Laif: hemis.fr)
R. Austinat (1 bottom, 23, 30, 32, 34, 38, 56, 66, 69, 77, 85, 87, 94, 97); W. Dieterich (36, 44, 49, 62, 71, 93, 110 top);
EAT Restaurant (16 bottom); Getty Images/Flickr: Hal Bergman Photography (57); Getty Images/Photodisc: Mahaux
(24 right); Huber: Canali (24 left), Hallberg (54/55), Huber (10/11, 137), Kremer (front flap left, 122/123); © iStockphoto.
com: John Kropewnicki (17 bottom); Laif: hemis.fr (1 top); Laif/hemis.fr: Renault (100); Laif/Polaris: Tambunan
(107); Laif/Redux/The New York Times: DaSilva (105), Randl L. Beach (90), Wilson (3 centre, 5, 78, 80/81, 106/107);
Laif/Redux: Drew Kelly (68 right); Laif: Falke (front flap right), hemis.fr (1 top), Modrow (12/13, 25), Perousse (41,
65, 82), Redux (74); UPI (106); Look: Age Fotostock (47, 58), Fleisher (15), Martini (42); mauritius images/Age
Fotostock: Hamilton (20); mauritius images/imagebroker: Kohls (46); mauritius images: AGE (6), Alamy (52,
104), Fagot (2 centre bottom, 26/27), Foodpix (68 left), Kinne (3 bottom, 88/89), Scott (98/99), Unverzagt (16/17);
Mission Bicycle: Zachary Rosen (16 centre); pARADOX aRTS: Lori B Bloustein (17 top); Reware Style: emiko-o (16 top);
T. Stankiewicz (16 bottom, 3 top, 7, 9, 50, 60/61, 72/73, 110 bottom, 111); vario images: Etsabild (104/105), imagebroker
(2 centre top, 8), McPHOTO (2 top, 4, 102), RHPL (103)

1st Edition 2012
Worldwide Distribution: Marco Polo Travel Publishing Ltd, Pinewood, Chineham Business Park,
Crockford Lane, Basingstoke, Hampshire RG24 8AL, United Kingdom. Email: sales@marcopolouk.com
© MAIRDUMONT GmbH & Co. KG, Ostfildern
Chief editors: Michaela Lienemann (concept, managing editor), Marion Zorn (concept, text editor)
Author: Michael Schwelin, co-author: Roland Austinat; editor: Marlis v. Hessert-Fraatz
Programme supervision: Ann-Katrin Kutzner, Nikolai Michaelis, Silwen Randebrock
Picture editor: Gabriele Forst, Barbara Schmid
What's hot: wunder media, Munich
Cartography street atlas: © MapMedia Corp., Toronto, ON, Canada M9W 1B3
Cartography pull-out map: © MAIRDUMONT, Ostfildern
Design: milchhof: atelier, Berlin;
Front cover, pull-out map cover, page 1: factor product munich
Translated from German by Robert McInnes; editor of the English edition: Christopher Wynne
No part of this book may be reproduced, stored in a retrieval system or transmitted in any form or by any means
(electronic, mechanical, photocopying, recording or otherwise) without prior written permission from the publisher.
Printed in Germany on non-chlorine bleached paper

DOS & DON'TS

How to avoid some unpleasant experiences

DON'T PARK YOUR CAR WITHOUT ...

turning off the engine, without putting it in gear, without using the handbrake *and* without turning the wheels so that they point towards the kerb (downhill tyres to the right, uphill to the left). The police are merciless about giving out parking tickets if the wheels are not pointing in the right direction.

DON'T RING THE BELL YOURSELF

The bell ropes in the cable cars are only for the *gripman* and *conductor*. If you want to get off, call out loudly and clearly: 'Next stop, please!'

DON'T SMOKE

The health craze has made itself felt even more strongly on the west coast than on the east. Smoking is absolutely forbidden in restaurants and bars.

DON'T FORGET YOUR ID

If you try to get into bars and clubs without any identification, you will not have any luck. And, if you buy something with your credit card, you will almost always be asked for your passport or other ID.

DON'T DASH TO A TABLE

Even basic restaurants have a *Please wait to be seated* sign at the entrance. A host or hostess then takes the guests to a free table when it has been cleaned and set. At some restaurants, you will be asked if you want a drink at the bar before dinner. You pay for it there before you go to your table.

DON'T PLAY THE HERO

If you happen to get held up, on no account should you offer much resistance. Those who threaten you are often hardened fighters and many of them don't shy away from violence. Precautions: carry your handbag diagonally across the front of your body or use a backpack or belt bag. Don't show that you have valuables on you and do not go for a walk in San Francisco's parks at night.

DON'T THINK SHOES ARE NOT IMPORTANT

Of course, Americans are usually rather relaxed. But the bouncers in many clubs and bars pay attention to guests' shoes – you should try to have a decent pair in your luggage.

DON'T BE STINGY WITH YOUR TIPS

In some countries, you only round off the bill but in the USA 15 percent is standard. The waiters often work for a pittance and employers only rarely pay their health insurance. If the service is really good – or really bad – adjust the tip accordingly.